When the day comes when courses in life and sanity are taught in all our schools, Wendell Berry's book, **THE LONG-LEGGED HOUSE,** should be the chosen text.

—Josephine Johnson, author of "The Inland Island" in *The Nation*

There is a quiet strength and a deep challenge in the words of Wendell Berry. As one who has left New York to return to his farm in Kentucky, he calls on each of us to find the way to the place we care for and become a part of it.

Wendell Berry, teacher, farmer, and writer, was born in Louisville in 1934 and holds A.B. and M.A. degrees from the University of Kentucky. His poems have appeared widely in magazines and in four collections, *The Broken Ground, Openings, Findings,* and *Farming: A Handbook.* His poem "November Twenty-Six, Nineteen Hundred Sixty-Three" appeared as a separate volume with illustrations by Ben Shahn. He is also the author of *Nathan Coulter, A Place On Earth,* and the widely acclaimed *The Hidden Wound* (to be published by Ballantine this fall). He lives with his wife and two children in Port Royal, Kentucky, and is a member of the faculty of the English department at the University of Kentucky.

THE LONG-LEGGED HOUSE

Wendell Berry

AN AUDUBON/BALLANTINE BOOK
An Intext Publisher
NEW YORK

Some of the essays in this book appeared originally in *The Hudson Review*, *The Nation*, and *Religious Humanism*. "The Rise" was published, in a special limited edition, by The University of Kentucky Library. The lines by Ezra Pound are from *The Cantos*, copyright 1948 by Ezra Pound, and are reprinted by permission of New Directions Publishing Corporation.

Library of Congress Catalog Card Number: 69-12028

SBN 345-02189-4-125

This edition published by arrangement with Harcourt, Brace & World, Inc.

First Printing: March, 1971

Printed in the United States of America

AUDUBON SOCIETY
1130 Fifth Avenue
New York, N.Y. 10028

BALLANTINE BOOKS, INC.
101 Fifth Avenue
New York, N.Y. 10003

FOR MY STUDENTS

CONTENTS

I

THE TYRANNY OF CHARITY*

The furniture maker is at work in the shade of some box elder trees that grow on the slope of the roadfill out at the end of his yard. Two chair posts, held by a system of pegs and wedges as in a vise, are on the puncheon bench in front of him. He is cutting the mortises into which he will later insert hewn slats to make the back of the chair. He uses a sharpened screwdriver as a chisel, driving it with a heavy hand ax. Nearby is another sort of homemade vise, this one made by pinning the longer member of an inverted treefork into a mortise in another puncheon bench, so that the shape is roughly that of the figure 4. This he uses to hold pieces to be shaped with a drawing knife; he sits in a low chair at the end of the bench, holding his foot against the leg of the 4, by that leverage supplying the holding power of the vise.

From the tree in the woods to the finished chair, the materials are handled by no hands but the furniture maker's own. In the process he uses only a few simple tools: a crosscut saw, an ax, a hand ax, a drawing knife, an auger, a pocketknife, a rasp, and the screwdriver sharpened into a mortising chisel. He also has a press that he uses to set the desired curves into chair backs and rockers. One needs to see him at work in order to understand how adequately his patient crafts-

*1965.

manship performs tasks that are usually done now by machines.

While he works, four of his children, who have come there to the shady place with him, play with the tools he is not using or swing in the swings he has made for them in the box elders.

Held in such narrow focus, revealing only the man at work and the few primitive tools, the scene might be thought to belong to some happily simple time in the past. But it is not in the past, and it is not happy. It belongs to the coal country of East Kentucky in the summer of 1965; it belongs to the tragedy of that country and its people, and to the shame, acknowledged or not, of what some still like to call "the American way of life."

The furniture maker, who moved down onto the state road in the hope that he might sell some of his work to passers-by and travelers, lives in an old scale house once used by a coal company to weigh trucks. The house is built of rough-sawed lumber, covered with the rather flimsy material called brick siding; it has had no upkeep for years, and one can see that in cold weather it must be difficult to heat. The yard is partly a fill of coal rubble, dumped and leveled around the house, which stands bare in the hot sun. It is the most meager home site imaginable, starkly and heavily ugly, sterile and coal-stained and raw. The children who play and swing there in the shade are poorly clothed. Only the seven-year-old girl attends school, but the furniture maker and his wife will be dependent again this fall on the uneasy charity that gives away secondhand clothes. The furniture maker speaks of his distress over the presence of a "store" in the child's school. The store sells popsicles and candy and such to the children, and it is one of the furniture maker's cruel burdens, for it requires him either to send the child to school with nickels he can't afford or to have the family's poverty made painfully obvious to her—and all her classmates—every day.

Unable to live by his work, the furniture maker is dependent on the government's welfare program, the benefits of which are somewhat questionable, since if he sells any of his work his welfare payments are diminished accordingly, and so he stands little or no chance of improving his situation by his own effort. Only the workman's loving pride in his work can explain why he has continued to make any effort at all.

Getting out of the car there at the edge of the road, standing up to face that black yard and the bitter shambles of a house, you are inclined to forget the good you know of the place, and to be overcome by a foreboding of hopelessness that by being theirs is also mysteriously yours. It becomes a strong temptation to get back into the car and drive away, to take refuge in the thousand lies we have invented to justify the divine right to be mindlessly rich.

But once you have come upon the furniture maker at his work this initial pressing of futility is, if not replaced, at least driven back by the excellence of the workmanship being accomplished with those crude tools in defiance of the poverty of place and circumstance. And this is supported by the sight of a large well-tended garden down in the creek bottom; the furniture maker is attempting to sell some of the produce in a makeshift stand beside the road, and his wife has been busy canning and preserving.

There comes the awareness, as it still must come here and there throughout the Kentucky mountains, that as a measure of the depth of misery there still remains a height of pride—a sort of last stand of hopefulness shaped in a neat garden, a few flowers in bloom. It may be only because of this that the misery itself does not yet represent the dead end of vision. One can bear the knowledge of the furniture maker's situation because there remains in the man himself the promise as well as the hope of something better.

Though the furniture maker's house and household wear the look of long poverty that is commonplace in

the region, there are significant differences between his
predicament and that of most. For while most of the
poor have become so because of the lack of employ-
ment, the furniture maker still applies himself indus-
triously to his work. And while most are handicapped
by lack of skills, the furniture maker is a consummate
craftsman. While the mentality of most has been con-
ditioned by a long dependence on coal company and
union, the furniture maker is self-employed and in full
possession of the discipline and pride of the craftsman
who is his own boss. And in a region, moreover, which
has suffered a thorough social upheaval in the change
from a dependence on the land to a dependence on
industry, the furniture maker came to his work by
inheritance. Asked how he learned his craft, he replies:
"It come to me from my ancestors."

The furniture maker's predicament is that though
he has work, it is work that is very near to being useless
and meaningless. He is prevented, as I have said, from
using it to augment his income from the welfare program. And he is bound to the program by his inability
to make a living entirely from his work. He lacks, for
one thing, a dependable market. Such furniture as he
makes is either not sufficiently valued by enough people
to assure a market, or the affluent passers-by who are
his potential customers simply refuse to believe that
anything of value could be produced in such a place.
For another thing, he is so slowed by his old tools that
he could hardly make more furniture than he does even
if he had more customers. It takes him, for instance,
about a month to make one of the large rocking chairs
that bring from seventy to ninety dollars. He can sell
only three or four of these a year, and most of his time
is taken up by articles from which he earns much less.

For fear that this will seem to anyone to be a senti-
mental defense of an anachronism, I hurry to say that
this man's work, particularly in his chairs, is among
the finest I have ever seen. The chairs are certainly the
strongest and best-made of their kind that I know of.

They are beautifully proportioned and balanced. Such ornamentation as is used is modest, and tasteful in a way that transcends fashionableness. They are made to last a lifetime and more, and their strength is achieved without expense of grace. It is hard to think of a room, rich or poor, that would not be dignified by the presence of one of them, and impossible to imagine a householder who would need to condescend to own one.

This, then, is an exceptional man. But if his troubles are not typical of the region, they are nevertheless indigenous to it, and are peculiarly revealing of the region's troubles. His fate cannot be separated from the fate of his land. Like every poor man in East Kentucky, he is suffering from the deficiency of schools and opportunities in a land sold out by the greed of its elected officials, and systematically plundered by the coal companies. If the truth were not already available to anyone who cares to know it in Harry Caudill's *Night Comes to the Cumberlands,* it would be almost mathematically demonstrable that a land of such wealth could have been reduced to such poverty only by fraud. (The region itself is *not* poor; the big money did not come there to get lost.) That the land and its people could have been so far brought down is explainable only by the failure of governors to govern and legislators to legislate and judges to judge in the interest of those they are sworn to serve—only by the subservience of our governmental ideals to the stupidity and greed of officials who have been willing to justify, by a spurious rhetoric of free enterprise, the right of the rich to get richer, by any means, at anybody's expense.

It is not possible to escape the irony of the fact that the furniture maker—a man of skill and industry, whose craft is itself one of the valuable resources of his region and nation, and who is engaged constantly in making products of great beauty and usefulness—is destitute in America, now. This, it must be remembered, is the very man whose promise the American government was established to redeem. By all our public claims he ought to be one of the prime beneficiaries of our system. As it is, he is its victim. And if *he,* with his skill and his devoted effort, has wound up under the heels of the exploiters, what hope can there be for those who are less able?

The reaction of good sense to this man's predicament can only be to ask: Instead of food stamps, why not tools? The food-stamp program, set up as it is to neutralize whatever income is earned by personal effort, is clearly stifling to ambition, making it certainly much easier, if not more remunerative as well, to do nothing. On the other hand, the few power tools that would be necessary to increase the man's productivity (perhaps enough to make him independent of government give-aways) would probably cost a good deal less than a year's supply of food stamps. The gift of tools, which would honor the capacity of the man to survive the troubles of his region and to support himself, would look toward a just end of the federal intervention in the region. The gift of food alone, whether or not limited to an established minimum, can lead only to an endless dependence on governmental charity—in which case charity becomes no more than a subtle form of oppression. If a man continues long in direct and abso-lute dependence on the government for the necessities of life, he ceases to be a citizen and becomes a slave.

The federal government has made no attempt to deal with the furniture maker in terms of his particular abili-ties and needs. And the Division of Arts and Crafts of the state government, which would be thought the most logical source of help, seems completely puzzled by him; his output is too small, the quality and price too high. The state seems prepared to encourage only such arts and crafts as can be mass-produced at dime-store prices. One gathers that the emphasis is entirely on sales, and that no consideration at all is given to the quality of the work or the integrity of the workman. The Division's sole impulse in dealing with the furniture maker is to "change" him—which is to say, to diminish and cheapen him. His only hope, the Division feels, is to reduce the quality of his work in order to raise the volume and lower the price, or make something more marketable—souvenir whistles, for instance. Nobody seems to have considered the possibility that it would be most natural, and even most expedient, to help him to make a living by doing what he already does supremely well. Nobody seems to know how he might get hold of some tools.

The truth is that the furniture maker is the dependent of his region in a more meaningful and crucial way than he ever will be the dependent of any government. And the measures that will lead to his recovery are those that will lead to the recovery of the region.

But at this moment East Kentucky is caught in the relentless grind of governmental cross-purposes. The federal government is there, carrying out various programs to assure that everybody will eat. Under the circumstances, that is commendable. But it is commendable only as a temporary expedient. To be worthy of admiration in any final sense, government help will have to accomplish the result of making itself unnecessary. It must be acknowledged both by the government and by the people that the charity programs can do no more than the minimum—can only prevent starvation. An agency or bureau or institution cannot exercise taste and judgment, cannot be motivated by love or compassion, cannot value a man for his industry or his art or his pride; they are abstractions themselves and must deal with people as abstractions.

To give a man bread when he needs a tool is as inept and unfeeling as to give him a stone when he needs bread, and this painful clumsiness is inherent in the generalizations of the social planners and the organized charities. Their most "humane" endeavors almost necessarily involve an attitude toward humanity that debases it. The tendency to deal with individual citizens exclusively in terms of the abstractions of their class or condition is to strike at the very foundation of American liberty, which was established to safeguard the possibility and the right of escape from such abstractions—the right to become exceptional. For the government to treat the furniture maker simply as one of the Appalachian poor is not only to insult and threaten him as an individual but to work at the destruction of the possibility that such craftsmen will ever live in the country again. To wage a "War on Poverty" in such a way as to encourage the exceptional to become ordinary would seem to imply an expectancy of defeat.

The furniture maker possesses the skill and the industry and the pride that make envisionable for him the personal triumph on which most of our ideas of human worth and dignity depend: the triumph of making a living in the work of one's choice, by one's own effort, by the use of one's own gifts. And this triumph is completely beyond the reach of any government or bureau. It cannot be achieved except by a man's own doing. What government *can* do—and this has always been one of the acknowledged functions of government —is to create and protect a condition in which personal effort is meaningful.

But having established and given extravagant publicity to the necessarily superficial expedient of feeding the hungry, the government seems to be doing little to bring about the economic health of the region. It can be said, in fact, that the government is tacitly abetting the further gutting of the region by the coal companies. The history of the greed and irresponsibility of these companies in East Kentucky does not need repeating. It only needs to be added that as this is being written strip mining is going on there at an unprecedented rate—in a silence of federal power that seriously threatens all corrective efforts of the state. And it needs to be said that this sort of mining involves not only the further departure of the region's wealth, with little or no benefit to the region, but also the irreparable destruction of the region itself.

In the face of this crisis, which demands prompt and

decisive action, the federal government has embarked on a two-year "study." For two years, then, nothing is likely to be done. And the bulldozers will grind on in a destructiveness surpassing that of any war or natural calamity; the mine owners will grow richer; the people will grow poorer; the possibilities of the region will be steadily and rapidly diminished. To anyone who has watched a strip mine being worked or has seen the results—the huge dead gashes in the mountainsides, timbered slopes inundated by avalanches of sterile over-burden, streams poisoned by acids and choked with rocks and mud, wells made unfit for use, the land and the homes of citizens destroyed—this two-year study is baffling and astonishing. It is not possible to imagine why it should take two years to "study" a situation that could be shown to be critical—to anyone with a live intelligence—in two days. Here again one smells the stench of the political fraud and bureaucratic paralysis that have begun to seem as natural to the region as coal.

Since the federal government is the largest customer (through T.V.A.) of strip-mined coal, and consequently the chief depressor of coal prices and the chief dis-courager of the less destructive deep mining, one must wonder if there is any real intention to do more for the region than to ask the best and the worst to come together to eat out of the government's hand.

THE LANDSCAPING OF HELL: STRIP-MINE MORALITY IN EAST KENTUCKY

"No!" interrupted the doctor. "There is no peace and no rest in the development of material interests. They have their law, and their justice. But it is founded on expediency, and is inhuman; it is without rectitude, without the continuity and the force that can be found only in moral principle."

Joseph Conrad, *Nostromo*

I have had quite a bit of trouble with this. I know what it means. Our homes are being destroyed . . . our wildlife destroyed, our peace destroyed . . . our dead rooted out of the grave.

Elder Dan Gibson of Fisty, Kentucky, at a hearing on new strip-mine regulations

At Frankfort, Kentucky, last August 25 and October 4 and 5,* there was a hearing on three new strip-mine regulations proposed by the Strip Mining and Reclamation Division of the Kentucky Department of Natural Resources. These new regulations were later adopted and put into effect, and now even stricter measures are pending before the present session of the state legislature. And so there begins to be some evidence that the state government has at last undertaken a serious interest in one of the state's most urgent problems. But since they face a powerful and determined opposition, the supporters of Governor Breathitt's new legislation

*1965.

12

might do well to consider the attitude and the morality displayed by the mining companies at the hearings of last August and October.

The proposed rules, as was made clear, were based on the careful research of trained men. Their purpose was to control—if not stop, then at least reduce—the erosion and water pollution that have so far been the inevitable by-products of strip mining. The gist of much of the testimony of the Division's expert witnesses was that the authors of the regulations had striven toward a maximum leniency. For instance, the table of standards that would regulate contour stripping of the steep slopes of East Kentucky was based upon a safety factor of one, which would assure control only under ideal conditions—the lowest possible safety factor. "To recommend a factor lower than one," a University of Kentucky professor of civil engineering testified, "is to recommend failure." It was also stated, without contradiction by the coal companies, that of the one hundred and twelve coal operations in East Kentucky all but twenty-two were at present working within the proposed limits as to extent of cut and degree of slope —which suggests that the regulations are lenient indeed.

But in spite of the minimal nature of the proposals, the opposition of the coal companies was inflexible and absolute. The company lawyers in their rebuttal made it clear that they would not be satisfied except by the defeat of even the least attempt to establish not only stricter controls but *any* controls whatsoever. They displayed no disposition to compromise, and no interest in discovering less destructive ways of mining. (Their witnesses indicated that the companies spend little or nothing on experimentation that might lead to less wasteful methods of extraction and reclamation.) The testimony of the expert witnesses who appeared in behalf of the companies was peculiarly clouded and disordered by the assumptions and intentions of the company lawyers, and by the testimony of several coal operators who also appeared as witnesses. There was a very obvious intent to use scientific evidence to prove that the best method of mining is the one that is most profitable, and that the best method of reclamation is the one that is cheapest. There was much yielding to the temptation to present theory and opinion as fact, and to look upon the failure to discover a remedy as proof that there is no remedy.

The testimony of one after another of the company witnesses turned on the same two arguments: (1) Any regulation that would reduce profit would be wrong; (2) control is impossible, in any case, because of the diversity of mining conditions ("every job is different"). I believe that most, if not all, of the scientists repeated the second argument, as if ignorant or oblivious of the moral and legal—and scientific—implications. One of them, F. A. Braley of Pittsburgh, a former member of the Ohio River Valley Sanitation Commission, testified that there is not much that can be done about acid water from the mines ("a very minor factor as far as water pollution is concerned"): "Best thing to do is pay for the fish that you kill and forget about it." And one of the engineers admitted that he had got his figures, in connection with an alternative proposal that would favor the coal operators, from the coal operators.

Instead of the proposed maximums of a solid-bench* width of sixty feet on a slope of thirty degrees, the operators almost unanimously asked for a solid bench of one hundred and seventy-five feet on a slope of thirty-five degrees. At least one of them suggested regulations that, under cross-examination, proved to be not only more lenient than the ones proposed, but even more lenient than the ones already in effect.

There was in the statements and questions of the coal company attorneys, and in the testimony of the operators, the unmistakable implication that anything can be justified by profit; that a man may own the land

*The "solid bench" is the horizontal plane of the cut in the mountainside.

in the same sense in which he would own a piece of furniture or a suit of clothes; it is his to exploit, misuse, or destroy altogether should he decide that to do so would be economically feasible. The question of the morality of any practice, for these men, has been completely replaced by the question of its profitability: if it makes money, it is good; if it makes money for *them,* they are doomed and eager to defend it. Evident in the testimony of some was the assumption that the steep mountainsides, now being ruined on an almost unbelievable scale and at great speed, are good for nothing else.

In short, the strategy of the coal companies was simply to ignore or redefine the issue. The issue, so far as the Division was concerned, was to determine how much control there should be. The coal companies hardly bothered to deal with that question. The issue they persisted in raising and speaking to was whether or not there should be any control at all.

At the close of the hearing one of the company lawyers rose to offer the "assurance" that, though the operators are working for profit, they do not wish to do so at the expense of the public welfare, or the welfare of their neighbors. They're concerned about the economic factor, he said, because they operate on a narrow margin of profit. There are a lot of irresponsible people in the coal business, he admitted, but he predicted reassuringly that those irresponsibles will bring about their own failure. He did not explain this process; presumably they will be dealt with by the same just and unerring Fate that so effectively deletes irresponsibility from the legal profession.

If the formalities and quibblings of the hearing room tended to diminish the urgency of the strip-mining problem, if the rebuttal of the coal companies seemed to imply that the issue of control was extremely debatable and surrounded by doubts, one had only to travel for a few hours on the back roads of East Kentucky to acquire a knowledge that would show the coal companies' self-justifications to be not only arrogant but vicious—and the Division's proposals to be mild.

Standing at the edge of the bench of a new strip mine on the mountain in back of the coal camp of Hardburly, one can look down into a narrow cove at a house that might reasonably serve as model and emblem of the predicament of the whole region. As mountain houses go, this is an exceptionally good one. It has been well cared for. There is a neat grassy yard with a hedge fence, and a garden. The slope above it has been planted in young pines. One can see, even from the height of the mine bench, that a man has taken a proud stand there, has put into the place the long and dear investment of his attention and love and work and hope; that because of the expenditure of himself there he has come to be in that place what he would not have come to be in any other place on earth. And one cannot stand there looking down without some sense of the great value, the great human potential—beyond profit making and productivity, and all our other fashionable and belittling sociological measures—of that man's response to the demands and attractions of that place.

But overhanging the house on three sides is the spoil bank of the mine. When I was there—in dry weather, soon after the cut had been opened—the spoil was already beginning to slide. As soon as the winter rains have soaked the ground, great masses of muddy spoil will begin to flow down the slope toward the house, destroying the timber and all the life of the mountainside as it comes. Since there is no natural law that protects the plantings and buildings of men, it is probable that the descending spoil will eventually destroy the stand of young pines, the garden, the yard, and the house itself. Or if the slide stops short of the house, the acid water from the opened coal seam will get into the well and make it unfit to use. It will pollute and kill the stream in the crease of the cove; where it once ran clear and glittering over the rocks it will begin to slide over a residue of mine filth—yellow, greasy-looking, stinking, utterly dead. Waters farther down will be polluted in their turn. And following the pollution will come the rubble and mud, filling up the stream beds, increasing the hazard of floods, destroying the health and the beauty of whole valleys. If the man of the house is not forced to move out of the danger of the sliding spoil, if in spite of all he chooses to stay, then he will live in a place as ugly and desolate as a city dump—the place, his life in relation to it, his hopes, his work, all as utterly destroyed as if bombed. And what then will his dreams be, and his hopes? How will he live then without a bitterness that will corrode and destroy him—and that none might dare hope would destroy only him?

Or one might drive up the valley road along Clear Creek at the foot of the same mountain—feeling the quietness and pleasantness of the pretty valley, and then coming aware of the presence in the tributary coves of the gray looming masses of spoil; coming aware that one is entering a doomed place—to see the story's end, not in prediction, but in fact: a house literally swept from the mountainside by a flow of mud and rubble from a spoil bank. And below the house, seeing the sterile earth and rock and splintered timber already cramming in to choke the little stream that runs there, one realizes that through its comely valley, Clear Creek already runs as dead as a sewer.

Or one can travel the Little Shepherd Trail, recently built along the backbone of Pine Mountain to attract tourists to see the natural beauty of Kentucky. But even there if one wishes to specialize in natural beauty one dare not look to the east, for on that side, paralleling the Trail for many miles, the most prominent feature of the scenery is a huge strip-mine scar in the side of Big Black Mountain. After one looks to the east the mountains to the west will seem to stand precariously in the same storm light that surrounds the bison and the whooping crane. To look east is to receive the poison of a doom that one did not expect at all to come upon in the woods.

Most of the mineral rights in the Kentucky mountains were bought up sixty or so years ago, long before present mining practices had become imaginable, for as little as a dollar an acre. If the price were all that was objectionable in those transactions, that alone would be cause to suspect any good intentions ever professed by the coal companies. But that is far from all.

Most of these purchases were legalized by deeds that conveyed, in addition to the ownership of the mineral, the right to build such roads, tipples, pit openings, et cetera, as would be necessary to remove the mineral from the property. The Kentucky courts have until now held that this right implies the right to strip-mine a person's farm or tract of timber without further payment. In other words, the surface rights on a piece of property, the mineral rights of which are held by a coal company, are now virtually worthless. At any time it pleases, the company may overturn the surface and whatever is on it—timber, croplands, buildings, roads, graveyards—without paying compensation or damages. And the point is not that this is legally possible, but that it is *being done*. Now, in the mountains of East Kentucky, it is common practice. The following complaint, printed in *The Hazard Herald* on September 30, is not unique, but typical:

> . . . they brought a scraper and pushed red dog from the road over into my garden and yard. When I got after them about this, they promised to get the red dog off my property and to replace my fence. My fence and fence posts are still lying flat on the ground where they left them. . . . One of their bulldozer operators unloaded his bulldozer right in the edge of my yard, drove it over a weeping willow tree that was about fifteen feet tall, breaking the tree off level with the ground. The men . . . told me that this . . . operator had been shell shocked in the war so he didn't know

any better. So one cannot help wondering if all of these men have been shell shocked as none of them seems to have any respect for the other man's property. Next, the culvert at Jack's Branch was stopped up, by mud, rocks, and trees . . . and flooded my barn, my pig pen, washed away a large stack of lumber, and washed out my chicken lot.

You can call their representative about all of this, and he tells you he has nothing to do with it. . . . Finally I managed to get a couple of calls through to this operator, but he practically makes fun of me for trying to get him to take care of the damage he has done to my property. I wonder what this man would do if someone treated him in the way he has treated me.

When the hearing was being held at Frankfort, a number of boulders (as large, it was estimated, as sixty tons) were allowed to roll off the bench of a strip mine into the vicinity of homes; three families were forced to move out for a time to avoid the danger. No warning had been given. (An officer of the company whose mine this was, testifying in Frankfort, said that it was "possible" that such incidents might have taken place, but he could not "remember" that any had.) At about the same time similar boulders were rolled across a county road at a time when a school bus might have been passing, again without any warning to anybody. One afternoon a housewife discovered, only by accident, that a blast was to be set off in a strip mine immediately above a road that a school bus would soon be traveling, and was able to call the principal in time for the children to be kept at school until the danger had passed.

The mining companies, then, have made it abundantly clear that they will destroy anything, they will stop at nothing, so long as the result can be inked in black on their accounting sheets. They have been abetted by the mischief and greed of local officials, by public indifference, by state paralysis, by federal cross-purposes and confusion. Against them there has been only a local organization of small landowners, the Appalachian Group to Save the Land and the People, headed by Leroy Martin of Hazard.

It has become plain that if there is to remain any hope at all for the region, strip mining, at least in its present methods, will have to be stopped. Otherwise, all the federal dollars devoted to the region's poor will have the same effect as rain pouring on an uprooted plant. To recover good hope and economic health the people need to have their land whole under their feet. And much of their land, seemingly beyond the reach of the bemused and fumbling powers that might have saved it, has already been destroyed.

To destroy a forest or an ecology or a species is perhaps an act of greater seriousness than we have yet understood. But given even a comparatively short time, these destructions will mend. The forest will grow back, the natural balances will be restored, the ecological gap left by the destroyed species will be filled by another species. But to destroy the earth itself is to destroy all the possibilities of the earth, among them the possibility of recovery. The land destroyed by strip mining is destroyed forever; it will never again be what it was; it will never be what it would have become if let alone. Such destruction—which can now be accomplished on a vast scale by a few men in a short time—makes man a parasite upon the source of his life; it implicates him in the death of the earth, the destruction of his meanings. Those men who send the bulldozer blades into the mountainsides bear the awesome burden of responsibility for an act that no one can fully comprehend, much less justify.

And though violence to the earth must seem in the long view to be the gravest of their offenses, one is also deeply troubled by their violence to justice. For do not all our rights have as their ultimate expression and meaning the right of a man to be secure in his own home? When this right is no longer defended by any power greater than himself, his days begin to come to him by accident, in default of whatever caprice of power may next require his life. When the possessions and households of citizens are no longer honored by the acts, as well as the principles, of their government, then the concentration camp ceases to be one of the possibilities of human nature and becomes one of its likelihoods.

The new strip-mine legislation that Governor Breathitt is asking the 1966 legislature to pass would, according to the Louisville *Courier-Journal,* "come close to making the coal companies leave the land in the shape they found it." It would require that, in mining operations on steep slopes, the overburden be piled back in the cut, rather than pushed down the mountainside; it would promote an interstate strip-mining compact to create uniform controls among the states; it would stop damage to private property and in other ways limit the surface destruction.

Today, before the enactment, and enforcement, of this legislation, some skepticism is still in order, but one must be encouraged by the apparent willingness of the Governor to risk measures based on an honest evaluation of the need. The new bills, if they are not so strict as some might have liked, are nevertheless more strict than might have been expected. They are too strict, they too willingly risk a bitter fight and the making of powerful enemies, to be merely a gesture. And so, in a state where political conflicts tend to be purely political, these bills give reason to begin to hope.

What is particularly hopeful about them is that they seem to be an effort by the state to pre-empt its own political and moral ground. If they are passed and enforced, we may be spared the necessity of a federal solution. And that—in a time when the federal government is often not only the ultimate authority but also the most immediate—is a most pleasing prospect.

No one, I think, welcomes the intervention of federal

power in the affairs of a state, except as a last resort. That seems the crudest of solutions. It is not a moral solution at all. In being forced to do what is right, men lose the dignity of being right. The right itself is debased as an aim and incentive.

A state solution to the strip-mining problem is, of course, less desirable than a personal solution. One wishes that the *persons* who own the mineral rights and run the mines had taken for themselves the prerogative of responsible and just behavior. If they had been willing to govern themselves strictly enough, it seems unlikely that they would now face the prospect of *being* strictly governed. But a state solution is, by the same token, more desirable than a federal one. The closer to home the correction is made, the better it is—the more moral it is.

Mining interests will, as a matter of course, bitterly oppose the new laws. They can be expected to argue, as they have before, that further controls will seriously impair the coal economy, and that to impair the coal economy will be to impair the economy of the state. Their moral poverty is shown by the fact that this, their principal argument, has already been publicly discredited. It is now generally known that, while their profits are enormous, their contribution to the state's economy is small. Their property taxes, for instance, are notoriously low, and Kentucky has not imposed a severance tax. That in the last three-quarters of a century coal worth billions of dollars has been mined in East Kentucky, with the result that the region is now a "depressed area," ought to testify sufficiently to the real nature of the coal industry's contribution to the state's economy.

Another danger, not so much to the passage of the legislation as to its ultimate effectiveness and meaning, may lie in the idea of "control." There is a possibility that the legislation can have it fullest meaning only as an intermediate step, leading toward a law that will abolish strip mining altogether. Nagging at the hope aroused by the Governor's bills is the fear that the idea of controlled destruction may be as much a rationalization, as potentially a delusion, as the idea of limited war.

Still another danger is the possibility that the proposed laws will be looked on simply as a local solution to a local problem. Their importance seems to me to be much greater than that. They represent what may be the most advanced effort on the part of the state to deal with the problem of strip mining. But more significantly, they are part of an effort, still young and faltering, to correct our abuses of the earth. They are part of an awareness that the earth belongs not only to us but also to our children. They take a stand against a crippling and peculiarly modern discrepancy between power and principle, the predicament of men whose use of the most powerful machines is governed by a morality that would be barely adequate to the use of a team of mules. The strip-mine issue brings to light only one of many monstrous possibilities created by the selfish use of principle—which is to say, contempt for principle—and by a moral climate in which a man can be, without discomfort to his conscience, *only* a coal operator, or only a doctor, or only a general.

In attempting to control the local activities of a few men, Governor Breathitt and his supporters have become, in fact if not by intention, the opponents of a widespread and widely respected set of attitudes toward life and toward the earth: the assumptions, inherited from the frontier, that the natural world is an enemy to be conquered and exploited, and that its riches are inexhaustible; the identification of economic license with poltical freedom, and the corollary that a free man is somehow morally obligated to get rich, his worth directly proportionate to his wealth; the willingness to be subsidized by posterity, to become rich at the world's expense.

POSTSCRIPT, JULY, 1968: A LAND
SET ASIDE

Early in 1966 the Kentucky General Assembly passed
a set of strip-mine regulations that I believe is still the
"most advanced" in the nation. At that time I felt some
hope that the state had at last determined to stand up
in behalf of its people, and to begin to correct the
ravages of a sin against the earth. But even then it was
clear that the new legislation, while a most necessary
and welcome first step, was by no means an arrival at
the promised land, and that, as a first step, it would
be virtually meaningless without further steps. Since
then two and a half years have passed, and nothing
more has been done. It has begun to appear that the
new strip-mine law, like so many laws in this country
in these times, has functioned as little more than a
diversion to draw attention away from a continuing
outrage.

In the mountains of Kentucky, as in the mountains
of other states, the irreparable cuts of the mines continue to be opened in the steep slopes, the sterile heaps
of spoil dumped onto the woods below, the streams and
valleys ruined, the people dispossessed, demoralized,
driven out. The overweight coal trucks still swarm over
the roads between mines and railheads in defiance of
the state's law, but with the tacit approval and con-
nivance of the state's lawmakers and law enforcers.
The coal, owned for the most part by absentee owners
in other states, still leaves the state untaxed. The
property taxes on coal holdings are still paid on the
basis of the most gentle of assessments. The coal country looks worse, more devastated and more hopeless,
than it did two and a half years ago, despite the new
law and despite the millions of dollars spent in the area

in the War on Poverty. And on June 21, 1968, the Kentucky Court of Appeals upheld the notorious broad-form deed, under the terms of which the strip miners—who own only the mineral rights, bought at scandalously low prices before strip mining had ever been thought of—have been permitted to destroy the farms and wood-lands and homes of the landowners without paying further compensation or damages. And so those who believed that the 1966 strip-mine regulations might loosen the death grip of the coal interests on the region are under an obligation to think again.

My most recent visit to the coal country of the eastern part of the state was at the end of July, 1968, and what I saw has filled me with a most oppressive and per-sistent sense of the smallness of human hopes before the inertia of institutions and machines.

On Frank's Creek in Letcher County I talked with Curtis Collier, whose story and whose seemingly un-avoidable fate represent, for me, the story and the fate of the region. The Colliers are people with an admirable mindfulness of their community. Across the road from his son's grocery store, Mr. Collier has donated land for a park, and has built some of the playground equip-ment himself. When I was there children were swinging in the swings. It is a shady, pretty place, and the Frank's Creek community is a pretty community. The houses along the road up the floor of the valley are nothing like the sagging soot-stained shacks that have become symbolic of the region—and that are indeed prevalent in the valleys and hollows that have had a history of coal mining. The houses along Frank's Creek are modest and decent and well kept. They stand in clean, lovingly tended yards, surrounded by flowers and trees and birdhouses. Nearly all have good, ample vegetable gardens. Here and there one sees little white colonies of beehives. The slopes of the valley are thickly wooded. In the small fields of the bottoms there are good crops of corn. There is everywhere the sense of amplitude and health—the sense that humanity has made a success here, and that an American promise has been fulfilled.

But now impending over this community is the knowledge that the slopes at the head of the valley, as well as some of the bottomlands, are soon to be strip-mined. Mr. Collier speaks out of a sense of doom gathering ahead of him. "Honey," he says, "it's going to be awful." Talking to Mr. Collier, and to his son and daughter-in-law in their store, one grows aware that a deep dread has entered into this place. The valley is tremulous with the anxiety of people about to face the death of what they have stood for and worked for and enjoyed—the death of their land, the death of their meanings. The familiar mountain has begun to loom over them as threatening as a volcano. When their valley is ruined, what will they do, where will they go, who will they be?

I rode with Mr. Collier over to some land he owns on Smith Creek, a tributary of Frank's Creek. We drove into a bottomland pasture of about ten acres, well grown in clover and grass. We looked at Mr. Collier's fat Angus heifers, and ate some blackberries from a briar growing in the fencerow. Mr. Collier showed me the barn that he had built himself and filled from floor to roof with hay from the little bottom. It is an attractive, well-used piece of land, and it is a part of the basis and support of the life of an attractive and admirable man; badly crippled sometime ago in a mining accident, Mr. Collier takes pride in having needed no one to help him.

But the strip miners have already opened two seams of coal in the slopes at the head of Smith's Creek, the stream has silted up, and Mr. Collier has begun a desperate and expensive effort to keep it from breaking across his pasture and destroying it. With the mountain torn open, there is simply no way of foretelling or limiting the damage that will be done by the heavy runoff from the rains of the coming winter.

It seems to me that Mr. Collier is a man of a kind that most Americans would claim to cherish and respect, a man of independent ability and pride and neighborliness. It is clear that American *ideals* stand very much in his support. But, I have been asking myself, what does the American *government* think of such a man? Will it sit by and see his land and his livelihood and his meanings all destroyed, and then offer him the benefits of the War on Poverty? Will it then expect to be congratulated for its foresight and beneficence? Will it consider that he has become more useful to its interests when he ceased to be one of the supports and fulfillments of its principles and has become its dependent'?

How, except by the utmost cynicism or indifference, can the government deplore the poverty and degradation of the mountain people while it permits, and connives in, the virtual extinction of their land?

In Perry County I drove to the mining camp of Hardburly, which has been the scene of a somewhat publicized community improvement effort. And since the time of my last visit there is a decided improvement in the looks of Hardburly. There has been a general cleaning and straightening, some of the houses have been painted, and there are a lot of flowers: lilies, dahlias, hollyhocks, zinnias, petunias, roses. But it seems a thwarted and superficial prettiness, for any amount of community pride in Hardburly would be overbalanced by the ravages of strip mining on the mountain above the town, and by the dead stream, as yellow with acid as urine, flowing beside the road.

From the town I drove on up the mine road to the top of the mountain, into the dumfounding waste that the strip miners have left behind them. I had been there before; three years ago I watched the bulldozers making the first cut into one of the now ruined slopes above the house and garden of yet another ill-fated mountain landowner. But it is impossible to remember it as it is; memory somehow refuses to accommodate the full dimension of the ruin. And standing there in the very presence of it, one feels one's comprehension falling short of the magnitude of its immorality. One is sur-

rounded by death and ugliness and silence as of the
end of the world. After my first trip to this place I think
I was most impressed by the extent of the destruction,
and its speed; what most impresses me now is its permanence. Generations from now these slopes will still be
a source of trouble and regret to the people who will
have to live on them or under them. Such land will pass
from generation to generation like a family curse, a
birthright of ugliness and shame and diminished hope.
Standing and looking down on that mangled land, one
feels aching in one's bones the sense that it will be in
a place such as this—a place of titanic disorder and
violence, which the rhetoric of political fantasy has ob-
structed from official eyesight—that the balance will
finally be overcast and the world tilted irrevocably toward its death.

Shall we encourage the planting of flowers in such
a place and feel that we have made just amends? Shall
we believe that a man dying of cancer can be cured by
wearing a bouquet?

As far as I have been able to see, the most legitimate
hope for the impoverished areas of the mountains lies
in the decent, modest, ample life of such households
and small farms as those along Frank's Creek. It has
seemed to me that the life of these places, still vitally
and meaningfully joined to the land, might furnish the
models and the inspiration for a renewal of the life of
the region as a whole. But anywhere that coal lies under
the ground, under the present laws, these houses and
farms and communities have no firmer hold on the future than so many bird nests. And when I look around
in the hope of some power that might save them, I see
only the state government carrying the coal industry on
its back like a winking uncle, and the federal government with its forms and rhetoric and half-answers, preoccupied by violence as though the destruction of Kentucky is to be compensated by the destruction of
Vietnam.

If the governments of state and nation want to do

more than prolong the death agony of the Kentucky mountains, then they must undertake the radical solutions that are necessary: a law forbidding any form of strip mining, at least on all sloping land and in all narrow valleys; a law to compensate fully all who have suffered from this type of mining and from the courts' misconstruction of the broad-form deed; an all-out effort to reclaim the lands already stripped; a property tax on coal holdings based on a full assessment of their present market value; a severance tax on coal. Without these measures all efforts to feed and clothe and uplift the poor will have the emptiness and futility of cynicism.

I must say that I do not see any reason to expect that any such corrective measures will be undertaken in time. I am having a great deal of difficulty in believing that either the state or the nation will meet its obligations in East Kentucky, and I am certain that the coal companies will be no more responsible than they are forced to be. I am afraid that the region has tacitly been made a preserve of the mining interests, to be exploited and destroyed to the last valley. I believe that the American system has already demonstrably failed in this region, and I am afraid that in the governments' refusal to acknowledge that failure and to act to correct it our system has begun a failure that is nationwide.

Since I left Hardburly I have been unable to escape the sense that I have been to the top of the mountain, and that I have looked over and seen, not the promised land vouchsafed to a chosen people, but a land of violence and sterility prepared and set aside for the damned.

THE NATURE CONSUMERS

We were awakened shortly after sunrise one Sunday morning by a woman's voice imitating a top sergeant over a public-address system. The amplifier was turned up to such volume that the sound seemed to come from all directions. The air was full of it. It could have been heard a mile away. Such a noise blasting into our sleep might have been alarming if it had not been so easy to guess the source: On the night before two cabin cruisers had tied up a hundred yards or so downriver from our house, and this was their method of waking up. That morning it had to be our method, too.

The P.A. system continued at full volume for maybe two hours: first the woman's strident sergeant imitation, waking up her fellow boatmen, and then radio music. Finally I went down to where the boats were tied and asked that the speaker be turned down, and was told by one of the boatmen: "We didn't know anybody lived around here."

There is no need to repeat all that was said, but the boatman made one other remark that surprised me. When I insisted that he had no right to create such a disturbance, he said: "We're on the *river*, you know."

I came home shortly after dark one night to see the light of a campfire on the shore of the river below the house, and when I stopped my car I could hear rock 'n' roll coming up from a radio. Several men, their boats moored at the shore, were sitting around the fire, drinking and talking, their conversation enclosed in music there as it would have been in a bar. I told them they were welcome, and asked only that they carry off their bottles and other garbage.

One of the men replied: "Why, *we're* boatmen."

His tone implied that my request was so unnecessary as to be insulting—that boatmen were not only respectful of the river but, as a group, *especially* respectful of it.

The next morning when I went back the boats were gone, and the rocks were strewn with bottles and with plastic and paper trash. The place had hardly been used, much less respected—it had been perched upon, befouled, ignored. Having spent the night there, those men doubtlessly did not recognize it on their way back.

I remember from two or three years ago a young couple who came to spend a vacation camping beside the river. Their car and camping trailer stopped on the road, and the young man got out. Even then he was wearing a pistol. He asked about a camping place, and I told him where to find one.

He made his camp on the riverbank, not far from the place where I came to work every day. He rented a rowboat from the man on whose place he camped, and the next morning went out on the river to fish. He was using the old-time leisurely equipment: pole and line, float, sinker, and hook. But he never stayed still long enough to fish. He rowed first to one place and then another and then another, the red-and-white float bobbing frantically in his wake. He could stay in any place no more than a few minutes, and when he moved he rowed with all his might. Now and then he rowed down to his camping place and called to his wife, who apparently would not leave the trailer. At almost regular intervals he drew his pistol and fired it—what at, I don't know.

For two more days he went on in that way, rowing the boat from one place to another in the same aimless

haste. He never did really fish. His wife never rode
with him in the boat. And at the same nervous intervals
I continued to hear the report of his pistol.

On the fourth morning he rented from the same man
an old speedboat, and spent the whole day trying to
make the motor run. He would pull the starter rope,
and make an adjustment, and pull the rope again. The
motor would start and run a few hundred feet—to whet
his appetite—and die. The sun burned down on the
river, and the day wasted, and he pulled the rope and
tinkered with the engine and pulled the rope.

The next day they were gone.

He had made clear the sort of vacation he wanted: a
simple, quiet, restful time in a natural place. But he
had proved as immune to that, as alien to the possibility, as if he had never thought of it. He had stayed
as remote from the place he had come to as if he had
never left the city where he lived. The longed-for time
had come, and passed: three days of terrible restlessness, and a day of terrible frustration. He has become
a symbol, to me, of an alienation from the world that
I believe to be common among us, and on the increase.
Because he could not be still, the place could not exist
for him. If his restlessness could have found expression
in horsepower—if he had had a motorboat that would
run—how many miles would he have traveled in those
few days? How many places would he have marked
with his oblivious passage?

Our house stands on a slope overlooking the Kentucky River a few miles from its entrance into the Ohio
at Carrollton. It has been a long time since this was a
"natural river." A system of navigation locks and dams
was built in the last century, and the land of the bottoms
has been as intensively farmed as any in Kentucky. Yet,
for those who know where and how to look, the valley
still has a rich natural life. In the summers we see wood
ducks and muskrats raising their young along the banks.
The great blue heron fishes here. In the woods on the

bluffs and around the slews there are still enough big trees for pileated woodpeckers to make a living. At night we often hear the awesome family talk of barred owls, or the barking of a fox. Occasionally we see deer. And beavers have begun to appear again on the banks of the river and its bigger tributaries where they were exterminated long before anybody now living can remember.

Here and there on the wooded slopes of the valley are tall open groves of a solemn beauty that keep, as if in a profound interior withheld from the ceaseless drone of engines, a fragment of the great quietness that two centuries ago lay upon the whole valley. The delicate flowers and mosses and ferns and the colorful mushrooms of the woods grow there. The voice of those places is that of the wood thrush, whose notes, without replacing the quiet, flow into it from some hidden perch —and into the hearing of whoever may be there, to attach itself like a clarifying emblem on the memory. In rainy times the streams step noisily and brilliantly down the rocky notches. If one can respond to the quiet of those places with quiet, and with enough attention, the woods will reveal its lives: squirrels and chipmunks leading the eyes into unsuspected places among the treetops and among roots and rocks and fallen logs on the ground; vireos and warblers singing and feeding in the dense foliage; water thrushes searching the edges of rocky pools.

Knowing this valley, once one has started to know it, is clearly no casual matter. Like all country places, it is both complex and reticent. It cannot be understood by passing through. It does not, like Old Faithful, gush up its inwards on schedule so as not to delay the hurrying traveler. Its wonders are commonplace and shy. Knowing them is an endless labor and, if one can willingly expend the labor, an endless pleasure.

I am not sure how one would judge a valley or compare it to any other. I guess that this one must be as attractive as most. To me, because I have been its inhabitant and intimate, it is the most attractive of all. I know that among all the other lives it holds and promises there is the possibility of rich hours and days and lives for people.

I have known this valley all my life. From the first it has been a source of pleasure to me, an object of interest and curiosity, an attraction. Every day I am here I learn more about it, and the more I learn the more clearly I see that my knowledge of it is one of its fragments.

The one part of its history that I have known from the beginning is the pleasure-boat era. Since the end of World War II motorboats have increased from rarity to such prevalence that on summer holidays and weekends the traffic is comparable to that on a highway. There are days when the river will not grow quiet from the wake of one boat before it is disturbed again by the passing of another, and these boats frequently travel in groups of a dozen or two.

The episodes that begin these notes are not typical of the behavior of vacationers on this river. But I think that they are symptomatic, and that they clarify some of the meanings of the boating phenomenon, and I am disturbed by what I think those meanings are.

The generalization that the activities of the boatmen tend to support is that, in relation to the natural world, the pleasure of Americans can be destructive in the same way that their work has already proved to be. It is not, certainly, a conscious destructiveness. But in that very unconsciousness it becomes an aspect of one of our worst national failings: our refusal to admit the need to *be* conscious. Or to put it more meaningfully: our refusal to admit that unconsciousness, in our time, is almost inevitably destructive.

The destructiveness of the boatmen is of a peculiarly modern kind. It is essentially the same as the destructiveness of certain industries, and it has the same causes: the use of powerful machines, and the discarding of more or less imperishable refuse. The destructiveness of the boatmen differs from that of industry mainly in the sad paradox that the boatmen destroy what they supposedly want to keep. They do not intend to exploit or damage anything. They have come to enjoy the river —and their enjoyment of it damages it. They do not use it as a fisherman uses it, leaving it as it was; they use it as clothing is used, leaving it always a little worse for the wear. They are the consumers of the river.

The aspect of this destructiveness that has attracted most attention, and has finally become the object of a state law, is the dumping of trash into the water. Of all the boating offenses this is certainly the most noticeable, and in many ways it is the most disgusting. An amount of trash that would be a relatively minor eyesore on a highway will deface the river for miles, carried and dispersed on the currents. One Fourth of July, while we ate a picnic on the riverbank, we watched a procession of bottles and cans and wadded papers from a lunch being served on a boat a few hundred yards up the shore. That sort of thing can give the open country a feeling of almost urban crowdedness. Much of the refuse that gets into the river is, of course, thrown in from the shores, and washed out of dumps by high water. But there is some that is just as certainly attributable to the boatmen. I have seen, for instance, whole table settings of paper and plastic dishes floating along together.

There is another concern that—because it has apparently received no attention, and because I am not a scientist—I can express only as a question: What effect is the turbulence of all this traffic having on the banks of the river? Of a wide river with gently sloping low banks this question would probably not need to be asked. But the Kentucky is narrow as navigable rivers go, its banks are high and extremely steep, and they are often composed largely of sand. Along such banks there will naturally be a continuous wearing by the current, but I think there is a reason to suspect that this natural erosion is now being hastened by the wake of the boats. The waves particularly of the larger boats strike with great force, leaving the water muddy and the wetted banks more vulnerable to the wake of the next boat. Some of the wearing in the banks seems clearly to have been caused by the lateral action of the waves rather than by the longitudinal flowing of the current. And there is some crumbling to be seen along the banks in times of low water, when there is no current but a heavy traffic of boats. Officials in Frankfort have told me that no consideration is being given to this problem. In view of the likelihood that the number of pleasure boats will increase steadily for a long time, it seems to me that some consideration *should* be given to it.

This worry is hardly a part of the boatman's experience. Speeding along, he has before him a tranquil river scene, peaceful and enticing as if pictured in a tourist brochure. When the shores begin to churn and the water to cloud with mud from the violence of his passing, he is not there.

But not only are the holiday boatmen often careless of the river—they monopolize it. There is no such thing, apparently as a slow pleasure boat. Even the large, awkwardly shaped houseboats are customarily equipped with powerful engines that send them along at cruiser speeds. When these boats take to the river in weekend numbers the pleasure of motorboating becomes the only possible pleasure. The use of a rowboat is possible, but hardly pleasant; canoeing can even be dangerous. Fishing, from a boat tossing and beating in the turbulence a cabin cruiser can stir up in a narrow stream, is simply impossible. Out on the river in a canoe or rowboat, it would be dangerous to act on the assumption that any approaching motorboat will do the common courtesy of slowing down. It is rare that one will do it. And even courtesy is curiously thwarted by the fact that the violence of the wake of some boats increases as they slow down.

From the confluence of its headwater streams at Beattyville to its mouth at Carrollton, the Kentucky River is 255 miles long. On a summer holiday this much river could accommodate many hundreds of canoes and rowboats and fishermen and swimmers, who could share it quietly and in some isolation from one another—the quiet and the isolation being, I assume, the reasons one would go to a river instead of an amusement park. But a hundred or so of these fast motorboats, evenly distributed over the length of so narrow a river, will produce the effect of crowdedness, fill it with noise, and substantially reduce the pleasure and the safety of everybody else.

But suppose that the river is used not by a hundred of these boats but by several hundred, as it is on summer weekends and holidays. Suppose that some of these boats are broadcasting music or talk over amplifiers, as some do. Suppose some of them carry on their decks men and boys pot-shooting with rifles, as they frequently do. It will be seen then, I think, what a disproportionate share of the good of the river is taken by them. It is not that the boatmen *want* to take so much. It is maybe more troubling to reflect that they take it automatically, thoughtlessly, simply because they go fast and make so much commotion.

There is another destructiveness involved in this sport that is less easy to understand, but that once explained may help to explain the rest. The use of these fast and powerful boats is not only destructive of the river and of the pleasure of other people; there is a sense, it seems to me, in which it is destructive of the pleasure of the boatmen themselves.

I know that if one of these men were asked to justify his sport he would certainly say that there is pleasure in the ownership and use of a fine boat, and that there is a pleasure in speed. I would agree. Some of those

boats are indeed beautifully made; I understand the
satisfaction there would be in the maintenance and use
of one. And I also am a creature of the time and know
the pleasure of going fast.

But then another question is suggested: If the han-
dling and speed of the boat are the pleasures sought,
then why should these people not be content to go
round and round or up and down on a ten-mile course
near their dock? Why should boatmen from Cincinnati
and Louisville, who have the wide Ohio to maneuver
on, come to a comparatively remote stream like the
Kentucky that is narrower, crookeder and more difficult?

The only answer I can think of involves another pathetic paradox. They come in search of peace and quiet,
solitude, some restorative contact with the natural
world. Which is a little like going in search of a forest
with a logging crew. Once they have got it, they have
lost it. They come to seek the stillness of a natural
place, and their way of seeking assures the failure of
their search. They seek relief from restlessness and
anxiety in these expensive, fast, superhorsepowered
boats, which are embodiments of restlessness and anxiety. They go toward their desire with such violence
of haste that they can never arrive. They go to the
country to rest, only to reproduce there the noise, haste,
confusion—and, surely, the frustration—of city traffic.

The boatman's pursuit of pleasure is determined and
limited not by his and his family's need but by the size
and speed of his boat, and so he takes far more than he
needs. It may be that he actually gets *less* pleasure because of taking so much. And the excess of his pleasure,
useless to him, is useless to everybody else. Because he
takes too much, he creates the possibility that others
will have too little. The boatman, then, has become what
more and more seems the ideal man of our society: a
superconsumer—which is to say, a waster, a ruiner, a
benefit to "the economy," a burden to the world.

The mentality that could support delusions so damaging to itself is strange to the world, alien to creation. It is like a dog that, chasing its own tail, catches it and bites it off. It is both a kind of madness and a kind of unconsciousness, so impenetrable by reason that I could not articulate the questions it raises, much less find answers, until I began to reflect on the two statements of the boatman quoted in the first of these notes.

We didn't know anybody lived around here. They had come, one must suppose, in answer to the summons, still much alive in America, that brought some men to the frontier: the attraction of a wild, uninhabited place. And the high wooded banks of this river had permitted an illusion that would have been dissipated by a glance at a road map, or even a moment's thought. *All* of Kentucky is inhabited now. The settlements have grown here for nearly two hundred years. The wild country is gone, along with the Indians and the buffalo and the wolves and the elk and the passenger pigeons and the parakeets and nearly all the old forests and much of the fertility of the land. Kentucky is inhabited all right, and for the most part the inhabitants have treated it as if it were uninhabited, or soon would be.

We're on the river, you know. He meant, of course, that he was in a public place, not my place, and so I had no right to complain. But I think he meant more than that. A wild, uninhabited place, such as he wanted to believe he had come to, is by the definition of our frontier experience a *free* place. One has no bosses there, one is free of responsibility and can do purely according to pleasure. How illusory that is is proved by the fact that the country *is* inhabited and that some of the inhabitants objected to anyone's behaving as if it were not. How illusory it is, and how dangerous, is proved by American history: Those pioneer forebears of ours, so attractively free of responsibility, not only settled the country but also used up the fertility and wealth and beauty of it at a rate that made their lives a disgrace to them and a burden to us. It is invariably damaging when men with neighbors act on the assumption that they are alone. And we are seeing with greater clarity and sorrow every day that the most solitary have had neighbors, and that the loneliest have had heirs.

What has troubled me most and longest is that these people, having come within reach of the decent harmless restorative pleasures that I know to be possible here, are oblivious to them, as remote from them as if they were looking at panoramic shots of the valley on a movie screen.

Propelled at twenty or thirty miles an hour by a roaring engine, one can experience the country only as "scenery"—a painted landscape without life or sound. "Scenery," as we speak the word, involves an oversimplification and falsification of nature. It is landscape with all the vital details excerpted. It is the notion that permits the indulgence of our wish to prettify nature— to pretend that nature is represented by butterflies but not mosquitoes, sunrises and sunsets but not hot noons, moonlight but not darkness, life but not death. But to know the mountain, as John Marin said, it is necessary to know what is on the mountain's back. One must go close and be still. And that cannot be done with a motor, or with a motorized intelligence. At twenty or thirty miles an hour the countryside can be no more than the pretty package a vacation comes in—to be used like other packages, disposed of as soon as the contents are used up. It is hardly to be kept in mind after it has been used, which means that it is likely to be used carelessly, or even contemptuously.

At night the roar of the engine is replaced by the radio. The watch fires of ancient travelers in the wilderness have their counterparts in the loudly playing radios of these modern voyagers. But it is no longer death that must be guarded against. It is life. What surrounds them now during their night stops is no longer the threat of attack by some enemy or large animal; it is nothing more than the life of the world as it is still serenely and persistently voiced in natural places at night in the sounds of the air and the water and the night creatures, each sound spaced, singled out, surrounded by a silence infinitely greater than it is, reaching to the stars.

It is maybe most of all that silence that they are so intent to guard themselves against. And there is indeed a potential of terror in it. It raises, still, all the old answerless questions of origins and ends. It asks a man what is the use and the worth of his life. It asks him who he thinks he is, and what he thinks he's doing, and where he thinks he's going. In it the world and its places and aspects are apt to become present to him, the lives of water and trees and stars surround his life and press their obscure demands. The experience of that silence must be basic to any religious feeling. Once it is attended to, admitted into the head, one must bear a greater burden of consciousness and knowledge—one must change one's life. If one has nothing in oneself with which to respond it would be unbearable. If the silence within the man should be touched by the impenetrable silence that ultimately surrounds him, what might happen to the thin partition of flesh and possessions? How might they have to be looked on then?

In the face of that silence—enmeshed as he most likely is in the demands of a life in which the prevalent motive is to take all you can get, and the ultimate check is everybody else's determination to do the same—no wonder he turns on the radio. No wonder he opposes the river by strewing on it his garbage and his noise. No wonder he goes as fast as he can. Pursued into the wilderness by questions he is afraid even to ask, no wonder he finds his comfort—to his bewilderment, surely—in what he thought he wanted to be free of: crowdedness and commotion and hurry and mess. He came to a natural place to be free of responsibility, only to receive from it the intimation that he cannot be free, that his life is surrounded by more demands and considerations than he can bear to admit.

Man cannot be independent of nature. In one way or another he must live in relation to it, and there are only two alternatives: the way of the frontiersman, whose response to nature was to dominate it, to assert his presence in it by destroying it; or the way of Thoreau, who went to the natural places to become quiet in them, to learn from them, to be restored by them. To know these places, because to know them is to need them and respect them and be humble before them, is to preserve them. To fail to know them, because ignorance can only be greedy of them, is to destroy them.

Nature has never permitted freedom from responsibility. The world is a most wakeful and exacting account keeper. Abusive and greedy lives are as certainly recorded on the face of the earth as they are said to be in the Book of Doomsday.

But that, the vacationing boatman seems often to conclude, is the world's fault, and to hell with it—and he dumps his breakfast plastic over the side.

The concern I have expressed here is justified less by the damage I have seen done than by the damage I believe certainly will be done if our minds do not change. For boating and the other mechanized pleasures, like everything else in our country now, are on the increase, both in the number of participants and in the power of the equipment. In all that I have said there is an apprehension of the question: If we continue our attempt to enjoy the world, as well as live and work in it, with our need for space increased by many horsepower, and our population getting always bigger, where are we going to find the room? Such a question is addressed not only to the possibility of control by law but to the consciences of persons. I do not believe that all of our abuses of the world can be stopped by law.

What I hope—and it is not an easy hope—is that people will begin to come into the countryside with a clearer awareness of why they come, of what they need from it and of what they owe it. I assume—and it is not an easy assumption—that the world must live in men's minds if men are to continue to live in the world.

II

THE LOSS OF THE FUTURE

We are a remnant people in a remnant country. We have used up the possibilities inherent in the youth of our nation: the new start in a new place with new vision and new hope. We have gone far toward using up our topsoils and our forests and many of our other natural resources. We have come, or we are coming fast, to the end of what we were given. The good possibilities that may lie ahead are only those that we will make ourselves, by a wiser and more generous and more exacting use of what we have left.

But we are still an exceedingly destructive people, and our destructions are still carried out, as they have been from the beginning, on the assumption that the earth is inexhaustible, and that we, the predestined children of abundance, are infallible. We live in a fallen world by the dangerous presumption that *we* are unfallen. Only a nation that is conscious of its own guilt can change and renew itself. We are guilty of grave offenses against our fellow men and against the earth, but we have not admitted that we are.

We must be tried now by the knowledge that what is at stake in our behavior is the world. The world is now our dependent. It is at our mercy. We have reached a point at which we must either consciously desire and choose and determine the future of the earth or submit to such an involvement in our destructiveness that the earth, and ourselves with it, must certainly be destroyed.

And we have come to this at a time when it is hard, if not impossible, to foresee a future that is not terrifying.

It is deeply disturbing, and yet I think it is true, that as a nation we no longer have a future that we can imagine and desire. The best we are able to hope for now seems to be to avoid chaos and obliteration by a sequence of last-ditch compromises. We have lost the hopeful and disciplining sense that we are preparing a place to live in, and for our children to live in. Instead of an articulate vision of a decent world, we have the bureaucracy and the rhetoric of the Great Society, an attempt through organization and wealth to delay or avoid the obligation of new insight, a change of ways, a change of heart. We do not believe in problems that do not have "practical" solutions. We have become the worshipers and evangelists of a technology and wealth and power which surpass the comprehension of most of us, and for which the wisest of us have failed to conceive an aim. And we have become, as a consequence, more dangerous to ourselves and to the world than we are yet able to know.

The great increase of our powers is itself maybe the most immediate cause of our loss of vision. It must be a sort of natural law that any increase in man's strength must involve a lengthening of his shadow; as we grow in power we are pursued by an ever-growing darkness. Our science has given us poisons that we cannot be trusted not to use against our land, or against our kind. Our mechanical skill has given us machines that have, as a necessary concomitant of the power to build, the power to destroy—and we have used them to destroy. Our power over the atom has made *us* the prospective authors of Doomsday, though it has not made us capable of guessing the full implications and requirements of such power. Even medical science, in addition to its benefits, must produce the horrors of overpopulation, and the hardly less troubling increase in the number of people who live beyond the pleasure of living. The anxiety is compounded by the doubt that man has ever possessed anything that he has not at some time made the motive or the means of his evil—or that he hasn't sooner or later put to the worst possible use.

Power has darkened us. The greater it grows, the harder it is for us to see beyond it, or to see the alternatives to it. It exercises as compelling an influence on us, who possess and use it, as it does on those we use it upon and against. In spite of all our official talk, now, about our high motives in Vietnam, most of us suspect that the only dependable explanation of our presence there is that we are strong enough to be there; for some, that seems also to be a justification. The rule, acknowledged or not, seems to be that if we have great power we must use it. We would use a steam shovel to pick up a dime. We have experts who can prove there is no other way to do it. A question that must trouble the rest of the world a good deal more than it troubles us is: Can we learn to use our power to avoid the doom of it? Has anybody—ever?

Along with the growth of our power, our history has acted to dull our sense of the future. Our history is not only the fund of inspiring events that in our obsessive self-congratulation we have made it out to be—it is also the record of a tragic and shameful wasting of the land and of human possibility. We have a past that has fed greedily and indiscriminately on our future. And the evidence is all around that the habits of the past are still present.

We come to the problem of the future, then, not with the endowments of a new nation and with all time before us, but handicapped by a history and a habit of waste, our power only doubtfully in control, and time turning against us.

Consideration of the future—which has become for us, now, so largely a question of self-control—leads necessarily to the consideration of ideals. Futurity and idealism are so closely involved with each other that, in my own mind, they function nearly as synonyms. The future is the time and the space and the ground of the ideal. The ideal, unless one believes in literal prophecy, is the only guide to the future. Men and nations who have no idealism—no order of hopefulness—have no future, or none they can bear to think about.

Our loss of any appealing vision of the future seems to me inseparable, in terms of both cause and effect, from our loss of idealism. Our public attitude has become political and cynical. Our political life is no longer effectively disciplined by any articulate political ideal. Though we talk compulsively—or our politicians do—of our high destiny and aims, the truth is that we no longer expect much in that line, or hope for much. We don't hope for much because our estimate of human worth and human possibility has dwindled. We don't expect much because we expect our leaders to be corrupt as a matter of course. We expect them, as we say, to be "realistic."

But one of the most damaging results of the loss of idealism is the loss of reality. Neither the ideal nor the real is perceivable alone. The ideal is apparent and meaningful only in relation to the real, the real only in relation to the ideal. Each is the measure and corrective of the other. Where there is no accurate sense of the real world, idealism evaporates in the rhetoric of self-righteousness and self-justification. Where there is no disciplined idealism, the sense of the real is invaded by sentimentality or morbidity or cynicism and by fraudulent discriminations. And that is a fairly just description of the present state of our national life. The voice of it, of course, is that of the television: a middle ground, a no-place, between the ideal and the real, where mental and moral discriminations are not only ignored but are less and less possible. War is funny. Sex is surreptitious, omnipresent, consummated only in advertisements. Stupidity is only amusing, as are such personal afflictions as speech impediments. Violence is entertaining, and manly. Patriotism is either maudlin or belligerent.

I cannot avoid the speculation that one of the reasons for our loss of idealism is that we have been for a long time in such constant migration from country to city and from city to city and from neighborhood to neighborhood. It seems to me that much of idealism has its source in the relation between a man and the place he thinks of as his home. The patriotism, say, that grows out of the concern for a particular place in which one expects to live one's life is a more exacting emotion than that which grows out of concern for a nation. The charity that grows out of regard for neighbors with whom one expects to live one's life is both a discipline and a reward; the charity that, knowing no neighbors, contributes to funds and foundations is, from the personal standpoint, only an excuse. It is patriotism in the abstract—nationalism—that is most apt to be fanatic or brutal or arrogant. It is when charity is possible only through institutions that it becomes indifferent, neither ennobling to the giver nor meaningful to the receiver. Institutional neighborliness can function as the very opposite of neighborliness, without impairing the moral credit or the self-satisfaction of the supporters of the institution. There is good reason, for instance, to suspect that the foreign mission programs of certain Christian denominations have served as substitutes for decent behavior at home, or as excuses for indecent behavior at home; in return for saving the souls of Negroes in Africa, one may with a free conscience exploit and demean the lives of Negroes in one's own community.

The breakup of our small communities and neighborhoods has produced a society of ghettos. I don't mean just the much-noticed ghettos of minority races and the urban poor. There are also ghettos of the rich, the intellectuals, the scientists, the professors, the politicians, and so on and on. These ghettos are not necessarily made up of groups living in the same place, but the people in them have the same assumptions, the same sort of knowledge, the same mentality, often much the same experience. They communicate mostly, or exclusively, with each other. Their exclusiveness and insularity foster the same homogeneity of attitude and the same self-protective psychology as any other ghetto. It is possible in the larger cities to live in a liberal intellectual ghetto, in which basic assumptions are rarely challenged or argued. It is possible to live in a university ghetto in which scholars and theoreticians converse only with other scholars and theoreticians in the same "field." Washington, one gathers, has a ghetto of politicians and a ghetto of bureaucrats—or several of each.

Those who by natural endowment and by training might have become the spokesmen and representatives of the ideal in our life have instead become specialists—experts in aspects. Those equipped by wealth or by power to bear great responsibilities have gathered into communities of themselves, insulated specifically against the claims of responsibility. What we have, as a result, are not communities but fragment-communities, the fragments communicating by means that can only be institutional.

But ideals grow out of and are corrected by the sense of the whole community and the individual's relation to it. There is no partial idealism. Specialists, answerable only to the requirements of their specialty, are remote from the possibility of idealism—hence, so far as the life and health of the community are concerned, they are without controls, particles in an expanding disorder. They are obviously and even notoriously prone to self-interest and to the perversion or misuse of their abilities. And they are indefatigable self-justifiers.

Anyone totally committed to a single pursuit almost inevitably becomes the propagandist of his own effort. As a nation of specialists, we have become a nation obsessed with self-justification. When we don't have it, we make it. And we are by now familiar enough with the make-work of manufacturers who need products, scholars who need projects, politicians who need issues, generals who need armies. We speak the language of a people bent on justifying everything we do or want to do, whether it is justifiable or not.

This preoccupation, with its consequent language of self-praise, is epidemic. It is chronic at the highest levels of the government. Much of the blame for the erosion of our idealism must be laid to the government, because the language of ideals has been so grossly misused by the propagandists. The liars of policy and public relations are addicted to a rhetoric of high principle. Our political ideals fill their mouths as unctuously, and with as little involvement of conscience or intelligence, as so many pieces of fat meat.

In the discussions over our war in Vietnam Senator Fulbright has asked whether we might be guilty of "arrogance of power." Even if one is disposed to believe in our innocence, it must be acknowledged that the question is of the sort that a moral people ought to be willing to bear against itself and to make the occasion of a strenuous self-appraisal. Instead, the President and others in the government have replied with repetitions of what they have always said, hardly varying the rhythm, and with insinuations against the character of Senator Fulbright—providing perhaps the clearest evidence so far that we have indeed become arrogantly powerful. We deal with what is surely the most relevant question that can be raised in a powerful country by ignoring it. We ignore it by using against it the language of our idealism, made so dogmatic and sanctimonious and automatic as to be proof against criticism, doubt, argument, even evidence—all that a live idealism must not only accept but invite. Our ears have been so dulled by such talk that we no longer notice how readily its voices slide from principle to self-righteousness and self-congratulation, and from that to personal slur. If one *subscribes* to high principles with enough fanfare, one need not act on them. So long as government speaks with a fervent idealism it is free to prolong its inertia and to indulge in expedient corruptions.

This eagerness to assure institutional survival at any

cost is apparent also in the churches, and most of the clergy speak an inflated high-toned language that is analogous in character and in function to the government's rhetoric. It is the language of a group mentality so perfectly certain of its rightness in everything that the answers are all implicit in the questions, and the questions in the answers—a language seeking the comfort of belief without alternative.

As a consequence of this fragmentation and vaporization of the ideal, reality becomes a sort of secular inferno in which nothing good is imaginable. This is the realism of many of our writers, but there is no reason to believe that it is only literary; it is a prevalent state of mind. When we look to the future we see no such visions as Jefferson saw; we see the cloud of Hiroshima standing over the world. We know, though we make it a desperate secret from ourselves, that in refusing the restraints of principle that might have withheld that power, we created not only an epochal catastrophe, but also the probability that it will happen again.

In a society of ghettos many of the vital labors of our duty to each other cease to be personal. They are necessarily taken over by institutions; the distances between the giver and the receiver, the asker and the answerer, are so great that they are simply no longer negotiable by individuals. A man living in the country or a small town might aid one or two needy neighbors himself; the most obvious thing for him to do would *not* be to phone some bureau or agency of the government. But what could he do if he were to try to exercise the same charitable impulse in an urban slum, or in Appalachia? The moral dilemma is suggested by a walk on the Bowery, equipped with common decency and a pocketful of change. What is the Samaritan expected to do when he meets, instead of one in need, hundreds? Even if he had the money, he would not have the time. Now, in America, I think he is likely to feel that he is expected to do nothing. He is able to reflect that there are organizations to take care of that sort of thing.

My point is not that these agencies do their work badly, but that having contributed to one of them, or even having heard of one, the citizen is freed of a *concern* that is one of the necessary disciplines of citizenship. And the institutionalization of charity has its counterparts in all aspects of our life, from the government down.

This usurpation of private duties by the institutions has fostered in the public mind the damaging belief that morality can be divided neatly into two halves: public and private. It appears easy now to assume that institutions will uphold and enliven the principles of democracy and Christianity, say, while individuals may without serious consequence pursue the aims of self-interest by the methods and the standards of self-interest. It is hardly necessary to say that men are commonly found who give passionate oratorical support—and, through the institutions, financial support—to the ideals of liberty and brotherhood, at the same time that in their private lives they behave and speak in ways antithetical to those ideas. It thus becomes possible to imagine the development among us of a society that would be perfectly hypocritical: a democratic government without democratic citizens, a Christian church among whose members there would be no Christians. In such a society it would be natural rather than disturbing for the exercise of patriotism to be taken over by investigating committees and the F.B.I. and the Pentagon, private conscience replaced by the Internal Revenue Service, governmental charity programs used to enrich the rich, churches used as social clubs and conscience sops for the dominant classes, ideals made the gimmicks of salesmanship, decent behavior adopted as the sham of campaigns.

The notion of a difference between private and public morality is, of course, utterly fraudulent—a way of begging every difficult question. Only men—separate, specific, one by one—can be moral. What is called the morality of a society is no more than a consequence of the morality of individuals. There is, by the same token, no such thing as a purely private morality, for the morals of private citizens are public *in effect,* and are increasingly so.

For some time now the government has been carrying on what it calls a War on Poverty. The government people speak of this program in tones which imply that it is the effort of a highly moral people. I do not believe it. Like some other current federal projects, it is a matter that the government talks about a great deal more than the people do. It does not contemplate any revision of our assumptions or our aims. It does not involve any change of heart or mind among the people of the country or the government. Uncritical of the powers and attitudes among us that have caused poverty, it can only cynically claim to hope to cure it.

There are a number of characteristics of the poverty war that seem to me typical of governmental high purpose. The government people have been congratulating themselves on it *from the beginning;* it may be that they reveal some doubt about it by being so unwilling to wait for results. The program has vastly elaborated and empowered the institutional presence of the government all over the country, and has vastly increased the number of people dependent on the government. It is an inspiration to freeloaders and grafters and chiselers. The program goes about its business with such fanfare, drawing so much attention to its own workings, that its specific effects are hardly noticed.

The worst is that the War on Poverty is a big generalization, giving suck to, and pregnant with, a great company of little generalizations. It has been made the occasion, for instance, of much squabbling among the social planners as to whose generalization about "the poor" is the most humane. What one hopes for is a beginning in the minds of those people of some suspicion that their generalizing may itself be inhuman.

It is not just or merciful or decent to treat people as abstractions. It is not tolerable to be treated as one. *Who,* and by what divine authority, determined that *all* who make under three thousand dollars a year are "poor"? Who except a robot would have the impudence to confront another man—a small farmer, say, with a garden, a milk cow, meat hogs, and an income of twenty-six hundred dollars a year, who farms because he *likes* to—with the news that, by a decree of his government, he is to be considered a pauper? Is there no sociologist or bureaucrat who can imagine how this sort of thing would sound to a man who is looking another man in the eye?

And so there are a number of developments in our society that have radically narrowed and darkened the moral space surrounding the individual life. That being true, and growth and change being now so nearly overpowering in themselves, it is perhaps not surprising that we have so little resistance to the temptation to think in terms of the expedient rather than the desirable, the temporary rather than the permanent, cures rather than preventions, painkillers rather than cures. Each problem or act tends to be isolated from all others, seen in terms of its own immediate conditions, related neither to principle nor to history, preyed upon by anxiety and by haste. To some extent this may be a necessary weakness of the institutional mentality, but this kind of thinking is apt to receive the acquiescence of most citizens, who accept "practicality" as the highest standard of public conduct. When the people have neither the incentive nor the moral means to resist and correct their institutions, they are poorly served by them. They become their servants' servants.

As more and more of the moral prerogatives of the individual are taken over by institutions and by agencies of the government, the individual does *not* become more secure and more happy. He becomes more confused, because moral standards in the hands of organizations will no longer answer the questions or illuminate the conditions of private persons. They become too generalized, too pumped up by righteous rhetoric, demanding too automatic and subservient an allegiance.

If the institutionalization of morals, as in the organized charities, involves a contradiction in terms, the same must surely be said of the legalization of morals, as in the civil-rights laws and the Medicare program and the issuance of government standards for business. The more explicit and detailed and comprehensive the law becomes, the more limited is the moral initiative of the citizen. It might be debated whether the citizen loses his moral prerogatives because they are "grabbed" by the government, or whether they are only *assumed* by the government after they have been abdicated by the citizen. In my opinion the latter is more likely: If the Thirteenth, Fourteenth, and Fifteenth amendments had been responsibly received by the people and the states, the recent civil-rights legislation would not have been necessary; if doctors had been more interested in service than in earnings, there might have been no need for Medicare; if the automobile makers had had either pride in their work or respect for their customers, perhaps they would not have needed to come to Washington, pleading their right to discipline themselves.

A more important concern, once it is recognized that citizens do abdicate their responsibilities, is *why* they do it. And how is it that some of those most guilty of irresponsibility turn up among the loudest advocates of freedom, and among the loudest objectors to "big government"? Freedom to do what? Instead of big government, what? It is certain, I think, that the best government is the one that governs least. But there is a much-neglected corollary: the best citizen is the one who least needs governing. The answer to big government is not private freedom, but private responsibility. If it is too late, as some think, for that answer to be given now, that is the fault of those who might have given it from the beginning, but refused to.

The most obvious reason for the abdication of personal responsibility in this country, I think, is the great difficulty of the ideals of Christianity and democracy that are most native to us. These ideals place an extraordinary moral burden on the individual as the result —and the reward—of their extraordinarily high estimate of the individual's worth. The follower of these beliefs finds himself in anxiety and trouble. If he loves his neighbor as himself, he has no reason to expect that he will not be hated in return. If he holds out for the political liberty of his neighbor, he has no assurance that his neighbor will not vote against him, or his principles, or even against political liberty. His convictions threaten him with the likelihood that he will have to act purely on principle—without certainty that the result of his act will be of practical benefit to him, without even the assurance that it will not be painful or costly to him— and that he will have to measure his life by standards so demanding that he must accept failure as a condition of effort. There is a sense, in other words, in which Christianity and democracy are moral predicaments. They propose an intellectual and emotional hardship, for which they do not provide either an easy solution or a handy comfort.

The typical reaction to this hardship is to take refuge in institutional formulas and regulations, to substitute reverential lip service and dues paying for the labor implied by the demands of the ideal upon the real. One imagines that there exists no greater potential of torment than in the minds of racist democrats or Christian militarists. That such as these are not noticeably prone to moral anguish is in my opinion owing almost wholly to the sanctified double talk characteristic of institutions. The same mentality that produced the notion of "Christian soldiers, marching as to war" now produces the notion of a "peace offensive." And in most of our talk about liberty and dignity our political institutions have permitted us to imply, with perfect consistency and propriety, the adjective *white*.

Another reason why we hold ourselves less and less accountable to our ideals is the habitual misrepresentation of these ideals to the young. Christianity and democracy are by definition problematic. Since it may reasonably be doubted that either has been fully and fairly tried by any society, they may even be considered experimental. They have so far produced more questions than answers. But they are commonly presented to the young *as solutions*—the packages in which all the problems of the human condition are neatly and finally tied up. Most Americans no doubt remember from their childhood the voices telling them: *All you have to do is vote. All you have to do is believe.* The problems of behavior and character and intelligence are all right, in their place. But what will lead the whole gang finally to the Promised Land, heaven on earth, or earth in heaven, is that pair of acts of brute faith. All that is needed is a consensus. The result is that the necessary stamina is not developed. The result is precocious disillusionment, weariness, cynicism, self-interest.

A third reason is that, in the minds of increasing numbers in the businesses and professions, the ideals of service and excellence have been replaced by the ethic of success, which holds that the highest aims are wealth and victory. To an alarming extent our schools and colleges are geared for the production of that kind of success, and are turning out graduates who not only do not desire any other kind but cannot recognize any other kind. Here is an ethic that can be clarified in a column of figures. It can be dealt with adequately by computers. It is made to order for everybody, except poor people and losers.

It is a bogus ethic because it is so specialized and exclusive. It is of use only to dominant groups. To the majority of the world's people it can seem neither an aspiration nor a justification. The wealth of some is always accompanied by the poverty of others. And it ought to be clear that where there are victors there must be losers. That we find these things so easy to ignore suggests how far our conscience has strayed into that middle ground where intelligence is impossible.

We have—as we were once eager to boast, but now reasonably fear—made a significant change in the human condition. Such power has grown into our hands that we must now look on ourselves not just as the progenitors but also as the *grantors* of such life as may continue on this planet. And in that a great deal is changed.

One might make a sort of formula: The growth of power increases the capability (and, apparently, the likelihood) of destruction, which must involve a proportionate increase of responsibility, which defines a need for a *developing* morality. That does not necessarily mean the continuous development of new moral principles. It does mean the continuous renewal of principles in the light of new circumstances, the continuous renewal and enlivening of the language of morality—to clarify, among other things, the identity of private and public responsibility.

Since 1945 it has been generally acknowledged that the world is our dependent. It has been acknowledged, that is, that it is the dependent of those governments capable of atomic holocaust. But it is becoming more and more apparent, as we continue to contaminate the soil and water and air and to waste and misuse the natural wealth, that the world is also the dependent of private organizations and individuals: corporations, contractors, developers, mining companies, farmers with modern chemicals and machines. Because of the enormous increase in the economic and technological power of individuals, what once were private acts become public: the consequences are inevitably public. A man on a bulldozer can scarcely make a move that does not affect either his neighbors or his heirs. All his acts, so empowered, involve a tampering with the birthright of his race.

The recognition of that amazing and terrifying dependence, and of the great difficulty of the obligation it implies, ought to make the beginning of a new moral vision, a renewal of the sense of community.

For too long the ideal role of the individual in our society—the role the talented young have aspired to almost by convention—has been that of the specialist. It has surely become as plain as it needs to be that what we need most now are not the specialists with their narrowed vision and short-range justifications, but men of sympathy and imagination and free intelligence who can recognize and hold themselves answerable to the complex responsibilities of a man's life in the world.

The failure of the modern cities, I think, is that they have become, not communities, but merely crowds of specialists and specializations. The businessman, the physician, the technician are specialists not only in the sense that they have become expert in narrow disciplines, but also in the sense that they accept the confinement of their discipline as the exact equivalent of the old idea of community responsibility or neighborliness. Thus the specialist who produces a drug or a formula or a technique or a machine may feel that he has done his "duty," no matter what use may be made of his work by others. The moral limits of his specialty are apt to coincide with his personal and selfish aims; what he has produced advances his career whether it advances the common good or not; his expertise and his self-interest slide smoothly together around him like the two halves of a capsule. Specialization, in this sense, is little more than a euphemism for moral loneliness; morally, the specialist is a man out of control, an erratic particle. The rioter in the black ghetto is a specialist of much the same kind, differing only in that he has not refused the obligation of neighborliness, but has been denied it.

The modern city, then, is in the fullest sense of the word a crowd, a disorderly gathering of people. Loneliness is on the rampage in it—so many separate lives pursuing their own ends among and through and in spite of the lives of all the others. And the disease that is destroying the community is destroying the families and the marriages within the community.

A community is not merely a condition of physical proximity, no matter how admirable the layout of the shopping center and the streets, no matter if we demolish the horizontal slums and replace them with vertical ones. A community is the mental and spiritual condition of knowing that the place is shared, and that the people who share the place define and limit the possibilities of each other's lives. It is the knowledge that people have of each other, their concern for each other, their trust in each other, the freedom with which they come and go among themselves.

Now it has become urgent that the sense of community should include the world, that it should come to be a realization that all men ultimately share the same place, the same nature, and the same destiny. But this most necessary feeling that the world is a neighborhood cannot, I think, be expected to grow among the crowds of strangers that fill the cities. If it is to be hoped for at all, it is to be hoped for among the people who have had the experience of being involved responsibly and knowingly, and at some expense of their feelings and means, in the lives of their neighbors.

Against a long-standing fashion of antipathy, I will venture to suggest that the best model we have of a community is still the small country town of our agricultural past. I do not mean that this was ever a perfect community, or that it did not have serious faults, or that it can be realistically thought of as a possibility that is still before us. But with its balance of variety and coherence, it is still more suggestive of the possibility of community, of neighborhood, than anything else we have experienced. Whatever may be said against it, it did bring into the condition and the possibility of neighborliness a number of people who varied a good deal in occupation, income, education, and often in opinion.

Different sorts of people, different kinds of experience and levels of education were in constant touch with each other, and were taught and disciplined by each other. Knowledge of neighbors was encouraged and cultivated, by the natural curiosity that produced either gossip or understanding, and also by the caution and interest of business dealings. A merchant or banker in one of those towns, dealing constantly with the problem of whom to credit, would in a lifetime gather up an authoritative knowledge of literally thousands of people. He gained from his business, in addition to his living, a profound and various experience of other men.

Though it was not inevitable, it was certainly possible in such a community for the life of a merchant or lawyer or teacher or doctor to be inspired and disciplined and even ennobled by a precise sense of its relation to other lives, its *place* among them, its usefulness and duty to them. Those places did not have the dead look of modern suburban towns in which the people live but do not work. The population was reasonably stable. People expected to remain in the same place all their lives, and often they did.

In those communities it was always at least possible that charity could be personal, and that possibility enforced the likelihood that it would be. A man whose neighbor was hungry would give him something to eat because it was the natural thing to do. He knew who his neighbor was. And he felt, without needing to be told by a sociologist, that the condition of his neighbor was a reflection on him. Because he knew his neighbor it was possible for him to care about him, or be his friend, or love him.

But the ideal community would include not just the living; it would include the unborn. It would be aware, with a clarity and concern which the best of us have hardly imagined, that the living cannot think or speak or act without changing the lives of those who will live after them. There would be a language, not yet spoken in any of our public places, to manifest and convey that awareness—a language that would live upon the realization that no man can act purely on his own behalf, not only because it is not desirable that he should do so, but because it is in reality not possible.

And it would include the place, the land, itself. For man is not merely "in" the world. He is, he must realize and learn to say or be doomed, part of it. The earth he is made of he bears in trust.

A STATEMENT
AGAINST THE WAR IN
VIETNAM *

I am a Kentuckian by birth, by predilection, and by choice. There are a good many people in this state whom I love deeply. And of all those perhaps only four believe that I should be speaking here today—and one of them is me. If that defines the difficulty of this speech, it also defines the necessity. I have received a dire warning that if I consort with such groups as this, I may be made a tool of "the Communist conspiracy." I don't believe that this warning was based on an accurate estimate of either my purpose or the group's. But having been warned, I think it only fair to issue a warning of my own: If there *are* indeed any communists in this audience, they should take care how they consort with *me,* for I intend to exercise an influence of my own and to subvert their aims.

I am deeply moved that today's meeting is taking place here in my State of Kentucky, for it means that the principle of thoughtful criticism and dissent, so indispensable to democracy, is alive here and may grow to be yet more alive. We are here because we feel that in the present grave circumstances our dissent and our criticism are more necessary to the health of our country than our acquiescence. We are here to become the voices, in this state, of the possibility of peace, which

*Speech delivered to the Kentucky Conference on the War and the Draft at the University of Kentucky, February 10, 1968.

we believe to be a better possibility than the possibility of war. We are here because we believe peace to be a better aim than victory, and peaceableness a better policy than belligerence, and charity more persuasive than strength, and brotherhood more intelligent than hatred. Perhaps—and not by our own intention—we are here also to test if the freedom of speech is alive in this state, and if Kentuckians have believed themselves free to speak only because they have had nothing critical to say. I am here because it is my faith that American political freedom is here, and because I believe that our countrymen of Kentucky, though they may not believe as we believe, will wish nevertheless to consider what we have to say.

I want to make clear at the outset that I am not an expert on any matter relating to the war in Vietnam. However, I have come to a most painful awareness that the possibility of life in the world is being threatened and diminished by that war, and by the attitudes that caused it and permit it to continue. Now that every war risks the doom of the world, I have come to the realization that I can no longer imagine a war that I would believe to be either useful or necessary. I have come to the realization that I am not comforted, and I do not feel secured in my hopes, by the knowledge that American planes are in the air, laden with the world's death. And having come to this understanding, I must now speak of it, for as an American citizen I understand also that the right to speak implies an obligation to speak.

I cannot claim that I speak for any organization, nor do I wish to. I do not "belong" to any organization, and I have put no institution in charge of my opinions. However, I do belong in the fullest sense of the word to a large *group* that is having a vast and ever-increasing effect on the world. It is known as the human race. I am aware that as a member of that group I am in the worst possible company: communists, fascists and totalitarians of all sorts, militarists and tyrants, exploiters, vandals, gluttons, ignoramuses, murderers, thieves, and liars, men for whose birth the creation is worse off and for whose lives other men will still be suffering a hundred years from now. The price of admission to this group is great, and until death not fully known. The cost of getting out is extreme. I find, therefore, no reasonable alternative to membership. But since I am a member on such exacting terms, I will not allow my involvement with this group to remain accidental, but will give my whole allegiance to it and work for its betterment. I will not be optimistic, for its history is full of ugliness and cruelty and violence and waste; it has inflicted terrible damage on itself and on the world. But I will be steadfastly hopeful, for as a member of the human race I am also in the company of men, though comparatively few, who through all the sad destructive centuries of our history have kept alive the vision of peace and kindness and generosity and humility and freedom—the sense of how comely and satisfying men's lives would be if they were all free and at peace, and if they cared enough for the world and for each other. It is in behalf of that vision that I wish to speak. I wish to be a spokesman of the doubt that the great difficulties of our time can be solved by violence. I wish to be a spokesman of the belief that the human intelligence that could invent the apocalyptic weapons of modern war could invent as well the means of peace.

I am opposed to our war in Vietnam because I see it as a symptom of a deadly illness of mankind—the illness of selfishness and pride and greed which, empowered by modern weapons and technology, now threatens to destroy the world. It is our fate that all of human history has reached a crisis in our time and in us. And though we inherit the attitudes and the habits and the conditions that have produced this crisis, we have not inherited the mental and the spiritual qualities that will be necessary to solve it; we must discover those resources in ourselves, and in our hope for the future. A. J. Muste said that for the early Christians "The past did not simply grind out the future through the sieve of the present . . . change and possibility were the operative concepts with which they worked." Do we think that peace is possible? If we do, then we must envision the particularities of that possibility. We must enact, and so substantiate, that possibility in our lives.

Our crisis rises out of an utter confusion about two fundamental questions: How should we behave toward one another? And how should we behave toward the world? These questions can be phrased in another way: What do we mean and intend by the idea that men have rights? What is our relation, in terms of dependence and responsibility, to the world? That we are confused about the answers is suggested by our reluctance to ask the questions. The questions propose a painful and humble labor of the spirit, and we would rather be confused. Our failure is a failure of imagination. In spite of our repetitious outrage at the violence in our streets and slums, we spend seventy per cent of our revenue on weapons—and so prove beyond doubt that we cannot imagine a better solution than violence. In spite of our constant lip service to the cause of conservation, we continue to live by an economy of destruction and waste, based on extravagance and ostentation rather than need; we can see no reason to be saving, because we cannot imagine the future of the earth or the lives and the needs of those who will inherit the earth after us.

We have been led to our present shameful behavior in Vietnam by this failure of imagination, this failure to perceive a relation between our ideals and our lives. We say that America is a nation founded upon ideals, and I believe that. I am a strong believer in those ideals because I think they offer the best hope for the chance of every person to live fully and to be free. But I am no longer able to believe that those ideals—or virtue or hope or decency or anything else that is desirable—can be advanced or preserved by force. That is why it sickens me to see us so willing to *fight* in order to influence the conduct of other nations. Why should *we*, who have splendid ideals and powerful arguments, rely primarily on violence rather than persuasion and example? Our almost exclusive reliance on force suggests to me, as I think it must suggest to the other nations whose friendship we desire, that we have lost faith in our ideals and that we know we have failed to live up to them. It is a commonplace that men fight when their arguments fail. It may be credible that a weak nation's arguments fail because of its weakness. But a strong nation's arguments fail because of moral default.

We say that America is a Christian and a democratic country. But I find nothing in the Gospels or in the Declaration of Independence or in the Constitution to justify our support of puppet tyrants, or our slaughter of women and children, or our destruction of crops and villages and forests, or our herding of civilians into concentration camps in Vietnam. We do these things because we have forsaken our principles and abandoned ourselves to the inertia of power. We have come to depend obsessively on an enormous capability of violence —for security, for national self-esteem, even for economic stability. As a consequence we have become blind to the alternatives to violence. This involves us in a sort of official madness, in which, while following what seems to be a perfect logic of self-defense and deterrence, we commit one absurdity after another: We seek to preserve peace by fighting a war, or to advance freedom by subsidizing dictatorships, or to "win the hearts and minds of the people" by poisoning their crops and burning their villages and confining them in concentration camps; we seek to uphold the "truth" of our cause with lies, or to answer conscientious dissent with threats and slurs and intimidations. The ultimate madness, of course, is that in order to destroy our enemies we are willing to build at great expense, and to keep in readiness, weapons whose use would inevitably destroy not only our enemies but ourselves and the world. All this is made frighteningly clear, in Vietnam, in our inability to control the swiftly widening discrepancy between what we are doing and what we *say* we are doing.

But I can best say why I am against this war by saying why I would be against any war. It has not yet been fully realized, and so it cannot be said too often, that the advent of the atomic bomb made a radical change in the human condition, and this change has been compounded by technological innovations of all sorts. Acts, modes of thought and behavior, that were tolerable twenty-five years ago are no longer tolerable. The smallest international conflict now palpably threatens to become World War III—which will not only be a war of men against men, but a war of men against the world, against life itself. It is now clear that men who turn in violence against their kind turn also against the creation. Surely the idea of a "limited war" is one of the most dangerously self-deceiving verbal gimmicks ever invented. For though war makes use of reason, as a weapon, it is not reasonable in nature. Its nature is the nature of pride and anger. It follows the brute logic of violent emotion, which points directly toward the use of the greatest available power. We should not forget that men have never possessed an instrument of destruction that they have not finally used. The atomic bomb—that "unthinkable" weapon that we claim to shrink from using—was, in fact, used *by us* before it had in any meaningful sense ever been heard of.

Wars have never made peace or preserved it or fostered its ideals. To have peace you must make peace with your enemy. To make peace only with your friends is to avoid the issue, and to permit a great principle to become absurd. Far from making peace, wars invariably serve as classrooms and laboratories where men and techniques and states of mind are prepared for the next war. World War II, for instance, in which we can say with some justice that we fought on the right side and for good reasons, made us a more warlike nation than we were before. Before it was over we had committed,

and made ourselves able to commit, acts of atrocity un-
imagined before. The unthinkable became thinkable because we became willing to think of it.

If I solve my dispute with my neighbor by killing
him, I have certainly solved the immediate dispute. If
my neighbor was a scoundrel, then the world is no
doubt better for his absence. But in killing my neighbor, though he may have been a terrible man who did
not deserve to live, I have made myself a killer—and
the life of my next neighbor is in greater peril than the
life of the last. In making myself a killer I have destroyed the possibility of neighborhood.

It is a mistake to believe that we only invest the
wealth and the lives of our citizens in war. We invest
their minds, too. We assume, dangerously, that minds
invested in war, and trained to be warlike, can, at the
signing of a treaty, be simply withdrawn from warfare
and made peaceable. But the training needed for peace
cannot be the same as that which is necessary for war.
Men cannot be taught and encouraged to kill by foster-
ing those impulses of compassion and justice and rea-
sonableness that make it possible to hope for peace.
The mentality of war, no matter how just the cause, is
the mentality of bloodthirst, anger, arrogance, hatred,
cunning, and passionate oversimplification. In fighting
a war, therefore, we are not preparing for peace, but
preparing, inevitably, for the next war.

One of the ugliest characteristics of modern warfare
is its almost exclusive dependence on the young—the
willingness to misuse young minds, to teach killing to
men too young to have fully understood what it might
mean to live, much less to kill or to die. The cynicism
of that is moral suicide. Why do we depend so on the
young to fight our wars? There is only one answer: The
young are persuadable. The young can be made to feel
in army camps and on battlefields what their comfortable elders are content to feel only in suburbs and
offices. If this government desires to do something in

the interest of peace, it might begin by raising the draft age from eighteen to forty.

But there is an argument against war that is yet more practical and apparent. It is that in the condition of war the two other major problems of our time, civil rights and conservation, cannot be adequately dealt with. It is obvious that war is the natural enemy of civil rights and liberties, and that, as its weapons and territories have increased through modern times, it has become increasingly destructive and wasteful of the lands involved and of their natural resources. No one any longer denies that the war in Vietnam is making it impossible for us to deal effectively with these other problems. The order of priorities is inverted and destruction is out of control; because of the urgencies of the war, temporary advantages appear more desirable than permanent values.

It is necessary for us to realize that when we speak of our reasons for opposing the war, we have already begun to speak of the great difficulty of the task of peace. Anyone who would undertake to hope or work for peace had better be fully aware of what he has against him. There is the same danger of oversimplification in the controversy over the war in this country as there is in the war itself. The fault of the President's widely advertised interest in peace is the weary nationalistic convention that all the wrong is on the other side: we are peace-loving, they are warlike; we are good, they are bad. I am unmoved by this sort of talk simply because I am not able to believe it. And I am no better able to believe the counterargument that all the wrong is on our side. I think that if we submit to the temptation to think in this way we will only be preparing yet another conflict, which yet other dissenters will see to be stupid and without justification.

Supporters of the war are constantly asking those who oppose it: Why don't you deplore the wrongs and atrocities committed by the other side? The answer, so far as I am concerned, is that I *do* deplore the wrongs and atrocities committed by the other side. But I am *responsible* for the wrongs and atrocities committed by *our* side. And I am no longer able to participate in the assumption that atrocities committed by remote control are less objectionable than those committed at arm's length. I am most concerned with American obstacles to peace because I am an American.

One of these obstacles, obviously, is our enormous military investment. It is the rule that when one has one's money invested in a machine, one does not wish to see the machine stand idle; the idleness of the machine means economic ruin. The United States is now investing seventy per cent of its money in a war machine. This means, however reluctant we may be to admit it, that we have become a militarist society; we have a vested interest in war.

Another obstacle is hypocrisy. Because we are a people with taxing ideals, and a normal love of moral comfort, it is perhaps understandable that we have evolved into an amazingly proficient set of hypocrites. And I think that a lot of our trouble is caused by our hypocrisy, which has blinded us to the difference between what we are and what we would like to be. A credibility gap exists not only between us and our government, but also between us and ourselves. Our ideals no longer serve us, because, though we probably talk about them more than ever, we no longer act according to them or judge ourselves by them.

But, it will be asked, can one *be* concerned with only one side of such a problem? If America were to become peaceable, and to live up to her Christian and democratic ideals, surely some warlike nation would destroy her. I do not know how to reply to that objection except to ask in return: Does the hope of peace lie in waiting for peace, or in being peaceable? If I see what is right, should I wait for the world to see it, or should I make myself right immediately, and thus be an example to the world?

And now I must ask: If a man believes as I have

said I believe, what should he do? The question is agonizing and I am not certain of the answer. But because I have children, and because I presume to offer myself to young men and women as a teacher, it is a question that I must ask. In the absence of better answers than I know, I must make myself willing to live with the question.

Clearly, those who disagree with the war policy have an obligation to say so. They have been entrusted with an idea and an argument. To me, that defines the function and the responsibility and the discipline of the peace effort: to advance the idea and the argument of peace. The main objective of any expression or demonstration by peace groups should be to articulate as fully as possible the desirability and the possibility of peace. I believe that a great danger to the cause of peace is the possibility that the peace movement might become merely negative, an instrument of protest rather than hope. Protest, necessary as it is, can only be temporary, for it is the creature of a political condition that is temporary. But the vision of peace is permanent; it has been with us for hundreds of years, and it is more meaningful and necessary now than it ever was before; it is only by this vision that the peace movement may hope to survive the war and remain relevant to our time and our predicament.

There are other dangers. There is the danger that the peace movement will be perverted by self-righteousness and disillusionment and anger. There is the danger that it will come to oppose violence with violence and hatred with hate—and so go over to the side of war after all. There is the danger that it will not be realistic enough, and so expect too easy a success, and so grow bitter. There is the danger that it will not be critical enough of itself, and so grow soft and proud.

There is the danger that we will begin to say, as some have said already, that because we face an extraordinary crisis we may be justified in behavior that would not be justified in a better time—that because our aims are high and our intentions good, we deserve the privilege of moral expediency. This is exactly the sort of moral finagling that permits men to fight "Christian" wars, and to kill one another in the interest of peace and brotherhood.

There is the danger that we will become anti-Vietnam or anti-Johnson *specialists*. Our obligation, once this impulse of peace has entered our thoughts, is to will it to grow and ramify until it affects all that we do. In seeking to change the world, we must see that we also change our lives. In promoting the cause of public peace, we should not neglect the equally difficult task of making ourselves peaceable. If we wish to oppose the government on the issue of war, let us make sure that there is a meaningful *difference* between ourselves and the government on that issue. The revolution that interests me and that I believe in is not the revolution by which men change governments, but that by which they change themselves.

For myself, I must say that I have little faith that we can improve ourselves or our condition merely by forming into organizations and drafting statements and giving public allegiance to principles. We have no right to hope for a better world unless we make ourselves better men. We must patiently and humbly seek out the causes of war that lie in our own thoughts and our own behavior, never forgetting that we are human beings, members of a war-making species. We must recognize that a dishonest or a wasteful or a violent life is as great a danger to the world as a weapon of war, and the violence of neighbors is the model for the violence of nations, and the hope for order in the world fails in a disorderly household.

Why am I against the war? I have two inescapable reasons. The first is that I am a teacher; the second that I am a father.

I am unable to teach on the assumption that it is part of my function to prepare young men to fit into the war machine—to invent weapons or manufacture them or use them, to write the oversimplified language of warfare or to believe it. As a teacher, I reject absolutely the notion that a man may best serve his country by serving in the army. As a teacher, I try to suggest to my students the possibility of a life that is full and conscious and responsible, and I am no longer able to believe that such a life can either lead to war or serve the end of war.

As a father, I must look at my son, and I must ask if there is anything I possess—any right, any piece of property, any comfort, any joy—that I would ask *him* to die to permit *me* to keep. I must ask if I believe that it would be meaningful—after his mother and I have loved each other and begotten him and loved him—for him to die in a lump with a number hanging around his neck. I must ask if his life would have come to meaning or nobility or any usefulness if he should sit—with his human hands and head and eyes—in the cockpit of a bomber, dealing out pain and grief and death to people unknown to him. And my answer to all these questions is one that I must attempt to live by: *No.*

SOME THOUGHTS ON
CITIZENSHIP AND CONSCIENCE
IN HONOR OF DON PRATT

I

The idea of citizenship in the United States seems to me to have been greatly oversimplified. It has become permissible to assume that all one needs to do to be a good citizen is to vote and obey and pay taxes, as if one can be a good citizen without being a citizen either of a community or of a place. As if citizenship is merely a matter of perfunctory dutifulness, a periodic deference to the organizations, beyond which it is every man for himself.

Because several years ago I became by choice a resident of the place I am native to, which I know intimately and love strongly, I have begun to understand citizenship in more complex terms. As I have come to see it, it requires devotion and dedication, and a certain inescapable bewilderment and suffering. It needs all the virtues, all of one's attention, all the knowledge that one can gain and bring to bear, all the powers of one's imagination and conscience and feeling. It is the complete action. Rightly understood, its influence and concern permeate the whole society, from the children's bedroom to the capitol.

But it begins at home. Its meanings come clearest, it is felt most intensely in one's own house. The health, coherence, and meaningfulness of one's own household are the measure of the success of the government, and not the other way around.

My devotion thins as it widens. I care more for my

household than for the town of Port Royal, more for the town of Port Royal than for the County of Henry, more for the County of Henry than for the State of Kentucky, more for the State of Kentucky than for the United States of America. But I *do not* care more for the United States of America than for the world.

I must attempt to care as much for the world as for my household. Those are the poles between which a competent morality would balance and mediate: the doorstep and the planet. The most meaningful dependence of my house is not on the U.S. government, but on the world, the earth. No matter how sophisticated and complex and powerful our institutions, we are still exactly as dependent on the earth as the earthworms. To cease to know this, and to fail to act upon the knowledge, is to begin to die the death of a broken machine. In default of man's personal cherishing and care, now that his machinery has become so awesomely powerful, the earth must become the victim of his institutions, the violent self-destructive machinery of man-in-the-abstract. And so, conversely, the most meaningful dependence of the earth is not on the U.S. government, but on my household—how I live, how I raise my children, how I care for the land entrusted to me.

These two poles of life and thought offer two different points of view, perspectives that are opposite and complementary. But morally, because one is contained within the other and the two are interdependent, they propose the same consciousness and the same labor. To attempt to interpose another moral standard between these two, which I take to be absolute and ultimately the same, is to prepare the way for a power that is arbitrary and tyrannical. To assert that a man owes an allegiance that is antecedent to his allegiance to his household, or higher than his allegiance to the earth, is to invite a state of moral chaos that will destroy both the household and the earth.

Since there is no government of which the concern

or the discipline is primarily the health either of households or of the earth, since it is in the nature of any
state to be concerned first of all with its own preservation and only second with the cost, the dependable,
clear response to man's moral circumstance is not that
of law, but that of conscience. The highest moral behavior is not obedience to law, but obedience to the in-
formed conscience even in spite of law. The government will be the *last* to see the moral implications of
man's dependence on the earth, and the *last* to admit
that wars can no longer be fought in behalf of some
men but only against all men. Though these realizations
have entered the consciences and the lives of certain
persons, they have not yet superseded the self-interest
of any government.

As law without conscience is hollow, so law that is
not willingly preceded and shaped by conscience is
tyrannical; the state is deified, and men are its worshipers, obeying as compulsively and blindly as ants.
The law is no defense against the greatest ills of our
time, for power, as always, subverts the law. Only the
consciences of persons can be depended upon to take
the stand that is unequivocally moral, and to make the
clear, complete refusal.

I do not mean to support, and I do not respect, any
act of civil disobedience that is violent, or that is ob-
structive of the rights of other people. Such overbearing
zeal is as fearful to me in the service of peace and
brotherhood as in the service of war and hate. But I do
support and respect those peaceable acts of disobedience
by which conscience withholds itself from the contami-
nation of acts antithetical to it, as when a believer in
the sixth commandment refuses to kill or to support a
policy of killing even when legally required to do so.
Such an act is no mere vagary. It is the basis and es-
sence of political liberty, defining the true nature of government as only such acts can define it—asserting, as
it has been necessary time and again to assert in the
history both of our country and of our species, that the

government governs by the consent of the people, not by any divine or inherent right.

To hear the boasts and the claims of some of our political leaders, one would think that we all *lived* in the government. The lower order of our politicians no doubt do so, and they no doubt exhibit the effects. But though I am always aware that I live in my household and in the world, I wish to testify that in my best moments I am not aware of the existence of the government. Though I respect and feel myself dignified by the principles of the Declaration and the Constitution, I do not remember a day when the thought of the government made me happy, and I never think of it without the wish that it might become wiser and truer and smaller than it is.

II

Nothing in my education or experience prepared me even to expect the horror and anxiety and moral bewilderment that I have felt during these years of racism and disintegration at home and a war of unprecedented violence and senselessness abroad. The attempt to keep meaning in one's life at such a time is a continuous strain, and perhaps ultimately futile: there is undoubtedly a limit to how long private integrity can hold out in the face of, and within, public disintegration. The conflict is plainly seeded with madness and death.

Even in our sleep some critical part of our attention is held by the descending roar of a machine bigger than the world—a society so automated and bureaucratized, so stuffed with the rhetoric of self-righteousness, that it is seemingly no longer capable of a moral or a human response. With the world in our power and our power assigned to the moral authority of those who will profit most by its misuse, we continue to bless and congratulate ourselves upon the boyhood honesty of George Washington. And so the machine descends. We are already suffocating in its fumes.

Slowly America wakens to the tragedy of her history, the unquieted ghosts of her martyrs brooding over her in the night, her forfeited visions, the plundered and desecrated maidenhood of her lands and forests and rivers. I write a little more than a week after the death of Martin Luther King, who lived as only the great live, in humble obedience to the highest ideals, in proud defiance of men and laws that would have required him to abide by a narrower vision and to dream a narrower dream. He stood for the American hope in its full amplitude and generosity. His martyrdom is the apparition of the death of that hope in racism and violence.

And today I live with the sorrow and shame that one of the finest young men of the university where I teach is in jail. He is in jail because he refuses to co-operate in the prosecution of a war that he believes to be unjust and unnecessary and immoral, because he insists upon living by the sixth commandment and the Golden Rule, because he does not believe that a wrong is any less a wrong when committed with the government's sanction and by the government's order. He is in jail because he will not acknowledge, because he cannot see, any difference between public morality and private morality. This young man's name is Don Pratt, a citizen of Lexington, Kentucky, a student of the University of Kentucky, one of the exemplary men of Kentucky. I acknowledge myself deeply indebted to him. His sacrifice and his fate have become a clarifying pain in my consciousness. His nobility is one of the reasons I have —and they are not abundant—to continue to hope for the future of my species. He and the other young men who have taken the stand he has taken are among the most precious moral resources of our country. Because they have not only believed in our highest ideals, but have also acted as they believed, the world is whole before them, and they are whole before the world.

There is, as Thoreau said, a great shame in going free while good men are in jail because of their goodness. Perhaps there is also shame in only going to jail while innocent people are dying or burning alive by the "accidents" of our technological warfare. There is shame in the inheritance of ancestral wrong, in the realization of how deliberately for how many years we have lived by the exploitation and waste of the earth and of one another. To open one's consciousness to the world as we have made it is to receive the sleepless anguish of this shame. To feel it is one of the costs to our kind of being morally alive.

And so, the sense of shame deep in me, and full of craving for moral clarity, I ask myself why it is that *I* am not in jail. And I answer, with much uncertainty, that I have not yet been faced with going to jail as an inescapable obligation—an obligation, that is, which would cancel out such other obligations as that of keeping together my family and household.

My life, as I have made it and as I understand it, is turned against what I consider the evils of our society—its suicidal wish to become a machine, its lethargic assumption that a mythologized past can serve as some kind of moral goal that can effectively discipline the present. My aim is to imagine and live out a decent and preserving relationship to the earth. I am determined to cling to this effort as long as I can maintain some meaning in it. But I know, the events of recent years make it clear, that there may come a time when it will be necessary to give it up, when to hold to it will be more destructive of it than to let it go. If I should be required in the name of the law to place my life in the service of the machinery of man's destructiveness and hate, then I hope for the courage to refuse in the name of conscience.

III

But wait. I am about to cross over into too much solemnity, a useless shame. Let me step aside from crowds—even the crowd of those whose opinions I share—and stand up finally in the place, and among

the concerns, of my own life. I wish to speak no further
except out of the few acres of hillside and woods and
riverbank near Port Royal, Kentucky, that I hope to
have made mine for life. I accept the meanings of
that place, for the time I will be there, as my meanings,
accepting also that my life and its effects belong in-
eradicably to that place. I am occupied there with a
small orchard, vines and berry bushes, henyard and
garden and pasture—with increasing the richness and
the abundance and the meaningfulness of that part of
the earth for my family and myself, and for those who
will live there after us. This effort has given me many
hours of intense pleasure, both in itself and in the sense
of what it means as a human possibility. It holds out to
me in the most immediate way the hope of peace, the
ideal of harmlessness, the redeeming chance that a man
can live so as to enhance and enlarge the possibility of
life in the world, rather than to diminish it. I do not
acknowledge the pleasure I take in this part of my life
with shame, though I know that while I have felt this
pleasure much of the world has been miserable.

The solemnity and ostentatious grief of some implies
that there is a mystical equation by which one man, by
suffering enough guilt, by a denial of joy, can atone or
compensate for the suffering of many men. The logical
culmination of this feeling is self-incineration, which
only removes one from the problem without solving it.
Because so many are hungry, should we weep as we
eat? No child will grow fat on our tears. But to eat,
taking whatever satisfaction it gives us, and then to turn
again to the problem of how to make it possible for
another to eat, to undertake to cleanse ourselves of the
great wastefulness of our society, to seek alternatives in
our own lives to our people's thoughtless squandering
of the world's goods—that promises a solution. That
many are cold and the world is full of hate does not
mean that one should stand in the snow for shame or
refrain from making love. To refuse to admit decent
and harmless pleasures freely into one's own life is as

wrong as to deny them to someone else. It impoverishes and darkens the world.

My impression is that the great causes of peace and brotherhood are being served these days with increasing fanaticism, obsessiveness, self-righteousness, and anger. As if the aim is to turn the world into a sort of Protestant heaven, from which all nonmembers have been eliminated, and in which the principle satisfaction is to go around looking holy. In short, the supporters of these causes are becoming specialists, like preachers and generals, and I think that is a very bad sign. Such specialists, it seems to me, are the enemies of their cause. Too many are now expending themselves utterly in the service of political abstractions, and my guess is that this is because of a growing sense of guilt and a growing belief that this guilt can be expiated in political action. I do not believe it, nor do I believe very much in the efficacy of political solutions. The political activist *sacrifices* himself to politics; though he has a cause, he has no life; he has become the driest of experts. And if he narrows and desiccates his life for the sake of the future of his ideals, what right has he to hope that the sucess of his ideals will bring a fuller life? Unsubstantiated in his own living, his motives grow hollow, puffed out with the blatant air of oratory.

What is happening now is that most public people, from government officials and political candidates to student activists, are involved in an ever-intensifying contest of self-righteous rhetoric. No one can feel certain he will be believed until he has said something more extreme than has been said before, and this both proceeds from and promotes the sense that the speaker is absolutely right and unimpeachably virtuous. There is no possibility of intelligence in it. And pacifists and peaceworkers especially should be aware of its enormous potential of violence. The problems of violence cannot be solved on public platforms, but only in people's lives. And to give the matter over to the processes of public rhetoric is to forego the personal self-critical moral intelligence that is essential to any hope for peace, and that can only function in the daily life of individuals. That I have abjured violence in principle does not mean that I have shrugged off the history of violence that I descend from, or the culture of violence that I have grown used to, or the habits and reflexes of violence in my body and mind, or the prejudices that preserve violence and justify it, or the love of violence. And this suggests to me that I can speak of my commitment to the cause of peace only with hesitance and with the greatest circumspection, and that I should avoid any rhetoric that might lead me to offer myself as a model.

IV

What one does can originate nowhere but in his life. If his life is organizational and abstract, dependent on the support and passion of crowds, full of the fervor of allegiance rather than the fervor of personal love and independence, then his love of peace is a hollow specialization. His hope is liable to be obscured by his cause. He is apt to find himself marching in protest against militarism and shouting or shoving in protest against force. The next step is only to join the militarists in making war in protest against war, soaring in self-righteousness, condemning and slurring all who do not agree. A tyranny of fanatical peace lovers is as credible to me as a tyranny of militarists, and I don't think there would be any difference.

It seems to me inescapable that before a man can usefully promote an idea, the idea must be implemented in his own life. If he is for peace he must have a life in which peace is possible. He must be peace-able. To be a peaceable man is to be the hope of the world. To be only an agitator for peace is to be a specialist, one in a swarm of random particles, destructive in implication, however pacific by intention. How can a man hope to promote peace in the world if he has not made it possible in his own life and his own household? If he is a peaceable man, then he has assured a measure of peace in the world, though he may never utter a public word.

I am struggling, amid all the current political uproar, to keep clearly in mind that it is *not* merely because our policies are wrong that we are so destructive and violent. It goes deeper than that, and is more troubling. We are so little at peace with ourselves and our neighbors because we are not at peace with our place in the world, our land. American history has been to a considerable extent the history of our warfare against the natural life of the continent. Until we end our violence against the earth—a matter ignored by most pacifists, as the issue of military violence is ignored by most conservationists—how can we hope to end our violence against each other? The earth, which we all have in common, is our deepest bond, and our behavior toward it cannot help but be an earnest of our consideration for each other and for our descendants. To corrupt or destroy the natural environment is an act of violence not only against the earth but also against those who are dependent on it, including ourselves. To waste the soil is to cause hunger, as direct an aggression as an armed attack; it is an act of violence against the future of the human race.

The American disease is the assumption that when a man has exploited and used up the possibilities of one place, he has only to move on to another place. This has made us a nation of transients, both physically and morally, and as long as we remain so I think that we will inhabit the earth like a plague, destroying whatever we touch. It seems to me that our people are suffering terribly from a sort of spiritual nomadism, a loss of meaningful contact with the earth and the earth's cycles of birth, growth and death. They lack the vital morality and spirituality that can come only from such contact: the sense, for instance, of their dependence on the earth, and the sense of eternal mystery surrounding life on earth, which is its ultimate and most disciplining context.

As long as a man relates only to other men, he can be a specialist with impunity; the illusion of the morality of "doing one's job," no matter what the job, is still accessible to him. But if he would establish a satisfying relation to a place, the capsule of his specialization must be broken and his commitments widen *perforce,* for the needs of his place, his part of the earth, are not specialized, and are as far as possible from the artificial, purely human contexts in which specialization is imaginable as a solution to any problem. Once he is joined to the earth with any permanence of expectation and interest, his concerns ramify in proportion to his understanding of his dependence on the earth and his consequent responsibility toward it. He realizes, because the demands of the place make it specific and inescapable, that his responsibility is not merely that of an underling, a worker at his job, but also moral, historical, political, aesthetic, ecological, domestic, educational, and so on.

V

What I am attempting to say is that what has come to be the common form of protest, in the anxiety and confusion of these times, is not the *only* form of protest, and that in the long run it is probably not the *best* form. I realize, of course, that there are some who have no alternative to public gestures of protest: demonstrations or draft refusal or exile. But for others there is the possibility of a protest that is more complex and permanent, public in effect but private in its motive and implementation: they can *live* in protest. I have in mind a sort of personal secession from the encroaching institutional machinery of destruction and waste and violence. Conscientious civil disobedience is the most familiar example of this, also the most dramatic, and surely all moral men must think of it as a possibility, and prepare themselves. But it is an extreme step, and in my opinion should be thought of only as a last resort. In addition to the personal sacrifice it demands, it removes one from other forms of protest; while one is involved in it, and in its consequences, one is by necessity a specialist of a sort.

Another possibility, equally necessary, and in the long run richer in promise, is to remove oneself as far as possible from complicity in the evils one is protesting, and to discover alternative possibilities. To make public protests against an evil, and yet live in dependence on and in support of the way of life that is the source of the evil, is an obvious contradiction and a dangerous one. If one disagrees with the nomadism and violence of our society, then one is under an obligation to take up some permanent dwelling place and cultivate the possibility of peace and harmlessness in it. If one deplores the destructiveness and wastefulness of the economy, then one is under an obligation to live as far out on the margin of the economy as one is able: to be economically independent of exploitive industries, to learn to need less, to waste less, to make things last, to give up meaningless luxuries, to understand and resist the language of salesmen and public relations experts, to see through attractive packages, to refuse to purchase fashion or glamour or prestige. If one feels endangered by meaninglessness, then one is under an obligation to refuse meaningless pleasure and to resist meaningless work, and to give up the moral comfort and the excuses of the mentality of specialization.

One way to do this—the way I understand—is to reject the dependences and the artificial needs of urban life, and to go into the countryside and make a home there in the fullest and most permanent sense: that is, live on and use and preserve and learn from and enrich and enjoy the land. I realize that to modern ears this sounds anachronistic and self-indulgent, but I believe on the ground of my experience that it is highly relevant, and that it offers the possibility of a coherent and particularized meaningfulness that is beyond the reach of the ways of life of "average Americans." My own plans have come to involve an idea of subsistence agriculture

—which does not mean that I advocate the privation and extreme hardship usually associated with such an idea. It means, simply, that along with my other occupations I intend to raise on my own land enough food for my family. Within the obvious limitations, I want my home to be a self-sufficient place.

But isn't this merely a quaint affectation? And isn't it a retreat from the "modern world" and its demands, a way of "dropping out"? I don't think so. At the very least, it is a way of dropping *in* to a concern for the health of the earth, which institutional and urban people have had at second hand at best, and mostly have not had at all. But the idea has other far-reaching implications, in terms of both private benefits and public meanings. It is perhaps enough to summarize them here by saying that when one undertakes to live fully on and from the land the prevailing values are inverted: one's home becomes an occupation, a center of interest, not just a place to stay when there is no other place to go; work becomes a pleasure; the most menial task is dignified by its relation to a plan and a desire; one is less dependent on artificial pleasures, less eager to participate in the sterile nervous excitement of movement for its own sake; the elemental realities of seasons and weather affect one directly, and become a source of interest in themselves; the relation of one's life to the life of the world is no longer taken for granted or ignored, but becomes an immediate and complex concern. In other words, one begins to stay at home for the same reasons that most people now go away.

I am writing with the assumption that this is only one of several possibilities, and that I am obligated to elaborate this particular one because it is the one that I know about and the one that is attractive to me. Many people would not want to live in this way, and not wanting to seems the best reason not to. For many others it is simply not a possibility. But for those with suitable inclinations and the necessary abilities it is perhaps an obligation.

The presence of a sizable number of people living in this way would, I think, have a profound influence on the life of the country and the world. They would augment the declining number of independent small landowners. By moving out into marginal areas abandoned by commercial agriculture, they would restore neglected and impoverished lands, and at the same time reduce the crowdedness of the cities. They would not live in abject dependence on institutions and corporations, hence could function as a corrective to the subservient and dependent mentality developing among government people and in the mass life of the cities. Their ownership would help to keep the land from being bought up by corporations. Over a number of years, by trial and error, they might invent a way of life that would be modest in its material means and necessities and yet rich in pleasures and meanings, kind to the land, intricately joined both to the human community and to the natural world—a life directly opposite to that which our institutions and corporations envision for us, but one which is more essential to the hope of peace than any international treaty.

VI

Though I have had many of these ideas consciously in mind for several years, I have found them extraordinarily difficult to write about. They are not new; other men have understood them better than I do. But there has not been much recent talk about them. Their language has been neglected, allowed to grow old-fashioned, so that in talking about them now one is always on the verge of sounding merely wishful or nostalgic or absurd. But they are ideas of great usefulness, and I am eager to have a hand in their revival. They have shown me a possibility and a promise beyond the dead end of going on as we are toward ever larger cities, in which ever more degraded and dependent and thwarted human beings stand in each other's way, breeding the fury of the world's end.

I am interested in the peace that is produced by politics because I believe that every day the holocaust is delayed gives the possibility that it will be delayed yet another day. But I am not exclusively interested in it, and I am not enthusiastic about it, because at best it is only temporary, and it is superficial, achieved always by expediency and always to the advantage of some and to the disadvantage of others. Political peace, like anything else political, is formed out of the collision of "interests," slogans, oversimplified points of view. And no matter how righteous the cause, it seems to me that a man is reduced by walking before the public with an oversimplification fastened to him. My evidence is that I have done it several times myself, and I never felt that I was doing what I was best able to do; I did not feel that there was any significant connection in what I was doing between my own life and the ideals and hopes I meant to serve. I was permitting shame to oversimplify what I thought and felt, so that I took too willingly to the crowd-comfort of slogans.

Political activity of any kind is doomed to the superficiality and temporariness of politics, able only to produce generalizations that will hold conflicting interests uneasily together for a time. But the life that attaches itself to the earth, to fulfill itself in the earth's meanings and demands, though it will certainly affect politics, will affect the earth and the earth's life even more. The land it has attached itself to will survive it, more whole for its sake. Its value will have the permanence of the earth, and be recorded in abundance.

Shame, like other hardships, must be borne. There is no handy expiation for the curious sense of guilt in having been born lucky, or in being well fed and warm and loved. To forsake life for the sake of life is to leave only a vacancy, all the old wrongs unchanged. Peaceableness and lovingness and all the other good hopes are exactly as difficult and complicated as living one's life, and can be most fully served in life's fullness.

VII

And so, difficult and troubling as the times are, I must not neglect to say that even now I experience hours when I am deeply happy and content, and hours when I feel the possibility of greater happiness and contentment than I have yet known. These times come to me when I am in the woods, or at work on my little farm. They come bearing the knowledge that the events of man are not the great events; that the rising of the sun and the falling of the rain are more stupendous than all the works of the scientists and the prophets; that man is more blessed and graced by his days than he can ever hope to know; that the wildflowers silently bloom in the woods, exquisitely shaped and scented and colored, whether any man sees and praises them or not. A music attends the things of the earth. To sense that music is to be near the possibility of health and joy.

Yet, though I know these things, I am still a member of the human race, and must share in its confusion and its fate. I cannot escape the knowledge that, though men are unable to attain the grace or the beauty of the merest flower, their destructiveness is now certainly equal to the world. Though I would only study the earth and serve it, I have not learned to escape a hundred empty duties and distractions that turn me against myself and implicate me in offenses against my own cause. Though I would sleep well and rise early, I lie awake in fear of evil. There is much of my life that I am not master of and that I see going to waste in bewilderment and subservience, lost in the driving storm of events and details.

What remains I commit to the earth.

III

THE RISE

We put the canoe in about six miles up the Kentucky River from my house. There, at the mouth of Drennon Creek, is a little colony of summer camps. We knew we could get down to the water there with some ease. And it proved easier than we expected. The river was up maybe twenty feet, and we found a path slanting down the grassy slope in front of one of the cabins. It went right into the water, as perfect for launching the canoe and getting in as if it had been worn there by canoeists.

To me that, more than anything else, is the excitement of a rise: the unexpectedness, always, of the change it makes. What was difficult becomes easy. What was easy becomes difficult. By water, what was distant becomes near. By land, what was near becomes distant. At the water line, when a rise is on, the world is changing. There is an irresistible sense of adventure in the difference. Once the river is out of its banks, a vertical few inches of rise may widen the surface by many feet over the bottomland. A sizable lagoon will appear in the middle of a cornfield. A drain in a pasture will become a canal. Stands of beech and oak will take on the look of a cypress swamp. There is something Venetian about it. There is a strange excitement in going in a boat where one would ordinarily go on foot—or where, ordinarily, birds would be flying. And so the first excitement of our trip was that little path; where it might go in a time of low water was unimaginable. Now it went down to the river.

Because of the offset in the shore at the creek mouth, there was a large eddy turning in the river where we put in, and we began our drift downstream by drifting upstream. We went up inside the row of shore trees, whose tops now waved in the current, until we found an opening among the branches, and then turned out along the channel. The current took us. We were still settling ourselves as if in preparation, but our starting place was already diminishing behind us.

There is something ominously like life in that. One would always like to settle oneself, get braced, say "Now I am going to begin"—and then begin. But as the necessary quiet seems about to descend, a hand is felt at one's back, shoving. And that is the way with the river when a current is running: once the connection with the shore is broken, the journey has begun.

We were, of course, already at work with the paddles. But we were ahead of ourselves. I think that no matter how deliberately one moved from the shore into the sudden fluid violence of a river on the rise, there would be bound to be several uneasy minutes of transition. It is another world, which means that one's senses and reflexes must begin to live another kind of life. Sounds and movements that from the standpoint of the shore might have come to seem even familiar now make a new urgent demand on the attention. There is everything to get used to, from a wholly new perspective. And from the outset one has the currents to deal with.

It is easy to think, before one has ever tried it, that nothing could be easier than to drift down the river in a canoe on a strong current. That is because when one thinks of a river one is apt to think of *one* thing—a great singular flowing that one puts one's boat into and lets go. But it is not like that at all, not after the water is up and the current swift. It is not one current, but a braiding together of several, some going at different speeds, some even in different directions. Of course, one *could* just let go, let the boat be taken into the continuous mat of drift—leaves, logs, whole trees, cornstalks, cans, bottles, and such—in the channel, and turn and twist in the eddies there. But one does not have to do that long in order to sense the helplessness of a light canoe when it is sideways to the current. It is out of control then, and endangered. Stuck in the mat of drift, it can't be maneuvered. It would turn over easily; one senses that by a sort of ache in the nerves, the way bad footing is sensed. And so we stayed busy, keeping the canoe between the line of half-submerged shore trees and the line of drift that marked the channel. We weren't trying to hurry—the currents were carrying us as fast as we wanted to go—but it took considerable labor just to keep straight. It was like riding a spirited horse not fully bridle-wise: We kept our direction by *intention;* there could be no dependence on habit or inertia; when our minds wandered the river took over and turned us according to inclinations of its own. It bore us like a consciousness, acutely wakeful, filling perfectly the lapses in our own.

But we did grow used to it, and accepted our being on it as one of the probabilities, and began to take the mechanics of it for granted. The necessary sixth sense had come to us, and we began to notice more than we had to.

There is an exhilaration in being *accustomed* to a boat on dangerous water. It is as though into one's consciousness of the dark violence of the depths at one's feet there rises the idea of the boat, the buoyancy of it. It is always with a sort of triumph that the boat is realized—that it goes *on top of the water,* between breathing and drowning. It is an ancient-feeling triumph; it must have been one of the first ecstasies. The analogy of riding a spirited horse is fairly satisfactory; it is mastery over something resistant—a buoyancy that is not natural and inert like that of a log, but desired and vital and to one's credit. Once the boat has fully entered the consciousness it becomes an intimate extension of the self; one feels as competently amphibious as a duck, whose feet are paddles. And once we felt accustomed and secure in the boat, the day and the river began to come clear to us.

It was a gray, cold Sunday in the middle of December. In the woods on the north slopes above us we could see the black trunks and branches just faintly traced with snow, which gave them a silvery, delicate look—the look of impossibly fine handwork that nature sometimes has. And they looked cold. The wind was coming straight up the river into our faces. But we were dressed warmly, and the wind didn't matter much, at least not yet. The force that mattered, that surrounded us, and inundated us with its sounds, and pulled at or shook or carried everything around us, was the river.

To one standing on the bank, floodwater will seem to be flowing at a terrific rate. People who are not used to it will commonly believe it is going three or four times as fast as it really is. It is so all of a piece, and so continuous. To one drifting along in a boat this exaggerated impression of speed does not occur; one is going the same speed as the river then and is not fooled. In the Kentucky when the water is high a current of four or five miles an hour is about usual, I would say, and there are times in a canoe that make that seem plenty fast.

What the canoeist gets, instead of an impression of the river's speed, is an impression of its power. Or, more exactly, an impression of the *voluminousness* of its power. The sense of the volume alone has come to me when, swimming in the summertime, I have submerged mouth and nose so that the plane of the water spread away from the lower eyelid; the awareness of its bigness that comes then is almost intolerable; one feels how falsely assuring it is to look down on the river, as we usually do. The sense of the power of it came to me one day in my boyhood when I attempted to swim ashore in a swift current, pulling an overturned

rowboat. To check the downstream course of the boat
I tried grabbing hold of the partly submerged willows
along the shore with my free hand, and was repeatedly
pulled under as the willows bent, and then torn loose.
My arms stretched between the boat and the willow
branch might have been sewing threads for all the holding they could do against that current. It was the first
time I realized that there could be circumstances in
which my life would count for nothing, absolutely nothing—and I have never needed to learn that again.

Sitting in a canoe, riding the back of the flooding
river as it flows down into a bend, and turns, the currents racing and crashing among the trees along the
outside shore, and flows on, one senses the volume and
the power all together. The sophistications of our age
do not mitigate the impression. To some degree it remains unimaginable, as is suggested by the memory's
recurrent failure to hold on to it. It can never be remembered as wild as it is, and so each new experience
of it bears some of the shock of surprise. It would take
the mind of a god to watch it as it changes and not be
surprised.

These long views that one gets coming down it show
it to move majestically. It is stately. It has something
of the stylized grandeur and awesomeness of royalty in
a Sophoclean tragedy. But as one watches, there ema-
nates from it, too, an insinuation of darkness, implaca-
bility, horror. And the nearer look tends to confirm
this. Contained and borne in the singular large movement are hundreds of smaller ones: eddies and whirlpools, turnings this way and that, cross-currents rushing
out from the shores into the channel. One must simplify
it in order to speak of it. One probably simplifies it in
some way in order to look at it.

There is something deeply horrifying about it, roused.
Not, I think, because it is inhuman, alien to us; some
of us at least must feel a kinship with it, or we would
not loiter around it for pleasure. The horror must come
from our sense that, so long as it remains what it is,

it is not subject. To say that it is indifferent would be wrong. That would imply a malevolence, as if it could be aware of us if only it wanted to. It is more remote from our concerns than indifference. It is serenely and silently not subject—to us or to anything else except the other natural forces that are also beyond our control. And it is apt to stand for and represent to us all in nature and in the universe that is not subject. That is its horror. We can make use of it. We can ride on its back in boats. But it won't stop to let us get on and off. It is not a passenger train. And if we make a mistake, or risk ourselves too far to it, why then it will suffer a little wrinkle on its surface, and go on as before.

That horror is never fully revealed, but only sensed piecemeal in events, all different, all shaking, yet all together falling short of the full revelation. The next will be as unexpected as the last.

A man I knew in my boyhood capsized his motorboat several miles upriver from here. It was winter. The river was high and swift. It was already nightfall. The river carried him a long way before he drowned. Farmers sitting in their houses in the bottoms heard his cries passing down in the darkness, and failed to know what to make of them. It is hard to imagine what they could have done if they had known.

I can't believe that anyone who has heard that story will ever forget it. Over the years it has been as immediate to me as if I had seen it all—almost as if I had *known* it all: the capsized man aching and then numb in the cold water, clinging to some drift log in the channel, and calling, seeing the house lights appear far off across the bottoms and dwindle behind him, the awful power of the flood and his hopelessness in it finally dawning on him—it is amazingly real; it is happening to him. And the families in their lighted warm kitchens, eating supper maybe, when the tiny desperate outcry comes to them out of the darkness, and they look up at the window, and then at each other.

"Shhh! Listen! What was that?"

"By God, it sounded like somebody hollering out there on the river."

"But it *can't* be."

But it makes them uneasy. Whether or not there *is* somebody out there, the possibility that there *may* be reminds them of their lot; they never know what may be going by them in the darkness. And they think of the river, so dark and cold.

The history of these marginal places is in part the history of drownings—of fishermen, swimmers, men fallen from boats. And there is the talk, the memory, the inescapable *feeling* of dragging for the bodies—that terrible fishing for dead men lost deep in the currents, carried downstream sometimes for miles.

Common to river mentality, too, are the imaginings: stepoffs, undertows, divers tangled in sunken treetops, fishermen hooked on their own lines.

And yet it fascinates. Sometimes it draws the most fearful to it. Men must test themselves against it. Its mystery must be forever tampered with. There is a story told here of a strong big boy who tried unsuccessfully to cross the river by walking on the bottom, carrying an iron kettle over his head for a diving bell. And another story tells of a young man who, instead of walking under it, thought he would walk *on* it, with the help of a gallon jug tied to each foot. The miracle failing, of course, the jugs held his feet up, and his head under, until somebody obliged him by pulling him out. His pride, like Icarus', was transformed neatly into his fall—the work of a river god surely, *hybris* being as dangerous in Henry County as anywhere else.

To sense fully the power and the mystery of it, the eye must be close to it, near to level with the surface. I think that is the revelation of George Caleb Bingham's painting of trappers on the Missouri. The painter's eye, there, is very near the water, and so he sees the river as the trappers see it from their dugout—all the space coming down to that vast level. One feels the force, the aliveness, of the water under the boat, close under the feet of the men. And there they are, isolated in the midst of it, with their box of cargo and their pet fox— men and boat and box and animal all so strangely and poignantly coherent on the wild plain of the water, a sort of island.

But impressive as the sights may be, the river's wildness is most awesomely announced to the ear. Along the channel, the area of the most concentrated and the freest energy, there is silence. It is at the shore line, where obstructions are, that the currents find their voices. The water divides around the trunks of the trees, and sucks and slurs as it closes together again. Trunks and branches are ridden down to the surface, or suddenly caught by the rising water, and the current pours over them in a waterfall. And the weaker trees throb and vibrate in the flow, their naked branches clashing and rattling. It is a storm of sound, changing as the shores change, increasing and diminishing, but never ceasing. And between these two storm lines of commotion there is that silence of the middle, as though the quiet of the deep flowing rises into the air. Once it is recognized, listened to, that silence has the force of a voice.

After we had come down a mile or two we passed the house of a fisherman. His children were standing on top of the bank, high at that place, waiting for him to come in off the river. And on down we met the fisherman himself, working his way home among the nets he had placed in the quieter water inside the rows of shore trees. We spoke and passed, and were soon out of sight of each other. But seeing him there changed the aspect of the river for us, as meeting an Arab on a camel might change the aspect of the desert. Problematic and strange as it seemed to us, here was a man who made a daily thing of it, and went to it as another man would go to an office. That race of violent water, which would hang flowing among the treetops only three or four days, had become familiar country to him, and he sunk his nets in it with more assurance than men sink wells in the earth. And so the flood bore a pattern of his making, and he went his set way on it.

And he was not the only creature who had made an unexpected familiarity with the risen water. Where the drift had matted in the shore eddies, or caught against trees in the current, the cardinals and chickadees and titmice foraged as confidently as on dry land. The rise was an opportunity for them, turning up edibles they would have found with more difficulty otherwise. The cardinals were more irresistibly brilliant than ever, kindling in the black-wet drift in the cold wind. The sight of them warmed us.

The Kentucky is a river of steep high banks, nearly everywhere thickly grown with willows and water maples and elms and sycamores. Boating on it in the summer, one is enclosed in a river-world, moving as though deep inside the country. One sees only the river, the high walls of foliage along the banks, the hilltops that rise over the trees first on one side and then the other. And that is one of the delights of this river. But one of the delights of being out on a winter rise is in seeing the country, and in seeing it from a vantage point that one does not usually see it from. The rise, that Sunday, had lifted us to the bank tops and higher, and through the naked trees we could look out across the bottoms. It was maybe like boating on a canal in Holland, though we had never done that. We could see the picked cornfields, their blanched yellow seeming even on that cloudy day to give off a light. We could see the winter grain spiking green over the summer's tobacco patches, the thickly wooded hollows and slews, the backs of houses and farm buildings usually seen only by the people who live there.

Once, before the man-made floods of modern times, and before the automobile, all the river country turned toward the river. In those days our trip would probably have had more witnesses than it did. We might have been waved to from house windows, and from barn doors. But now the country has turned toward the roads, and we had what has come to be the back view of it. We went by mostly in secret. Only one of the fine old river houses is left on this side of the river in the six miles of our trip, and it is abandoned and weathering out; the floods have been in it too many times in the last thirty-five years, and it is too hard to get back to from the road. We went by its blank windows as the last settlers going west passed the hollow eyes of the skulls of their predecessors' oxen.

The living houses are all out along the edges of the valley floor, where the roads are. And now that all the crops had been gathered out of the bottoms, men's attention had mostly turned away. The land along the river had taken on a wildness that in the summer it would not have. We saw a pair of red-tailed hawks circling low and unafraid, more surprised to see us than we were to see them.

Where the river was over the banks a stretch of comparatively quiet water lay between the trees on the bank top and the new shore line. After a while, weary of the currents, we turned into one of these. As we made our way past the treetops and approached the shore we flushed a bobwhite out of a brush pile near the water and saw it fly off downstream. It seemed strange to see only one. But we didn't have to wait long for an explanation, for presently we saw the dogs, and then the hunters coming over the horizon with their guns. We knew where their bird had gone, but we didn't wait to tell them.

These men come out from the cities now that the hunting season is open. They walk in these foreign places, unknown to them for most of the year, looking for something to kill. They wear and carry many dollars' worth of equipment, and go to a great deal of trouble, in order to kill some small creature that they would never trouble to know alive, and that means little to them once they have killed it. If those we saw had killed the bobwhite they would no doubt have felt all their expense and effort justified, and would have thought themselves more manly than before. It reminds one of the extraordinary trouble and expense governments go to in order to kill men—and consider it justified or not, according to the "kill ratio." The diggers among our artifacts will find us to have been honorable lovers of death, having been willing to pay exorbitantly for it. How much better, we thought, to have come upon the *life* of the bird as we did, moving peaceably among the lives of the country that showed themselves to us because we were peaceable, than to have tramped fixedly, half oblivious, for miles in order to come at its death.

We left the hunters behind and went down past a green grainfield where cattle were grazing and drinking at the waterside. They were not disturbed that the river had come up over part of their pasture, no more troubled by the height of today's shore line than they were by the height of yesterday's. To them, no matter how high it was, so long as the ground was higher it was as ordinary as a summer pond. Surely the creatures of the fifth day of Creation accepted those of the sixth with equanimity, as though they had always been there. Eternity is always present in the animal mind; only men deal in beginnings and ends. It is probably lucky for man that he was created last. He would have got too excited and upset over all the change.

Two mallards flew up ahead of us and turned downriver into the wind. They had been feeding in the flooded corn rows, reminding us what a godsend the high water must be for ducks. The valley is suddenly full of little coves and havens, so that they can scatter out and feed safer and more hidden, and more abundantly too, than they usually can, never having to leave the river for such delicacies as the shattered corn left by the pickers. A picked cornfield under a few inches of water must be the duck Utopia—Utopia being, I assume, more often achieved by ducks than by men.

If one imagines the shore line exactly enough as the division between water and land, and imagines it rising

—it comes up too slowly for the eye usually, so one *must* imagine it—there is a sort of magic about it. As it moves upward it makes a vast change, far more than the eye sees. It makes a new geography, altering the boundaries of worlds. Above it, it widens the freehold of the birds; below it, that of the fish. The land creatures are driven back and higher up. It is a line between boating and walking, gill and lung, standing still and flowing. Along it, suddenly and continuously, all that will float is picked up and carried away: leaves, logs, seeds, little straws, bits of dead grass.

And also empty cans and bottles and all sorts of buoyant trash left behind by fishermen and hunters and picnickers, or dumped over creek banks by householders who sometimes drive miles to do it. We passed behind a house built on one of the higher banks whose backyard was simply an avalanche of kitchen trash going down to the river. Those people, for all I know, may be champion homebodies, but their garbage is well-traveled, having departed for the Gulf of Mexico on every winter rise for years.

It is illuminating and suitably humbling to a man to recognize the great power of the river. But after he has recognized its power he is next called upon to recognize its limits. It can neither swallow up nor carry off all the trash that people convenience themselves by dumping into it. It can't carry off harmlessly all the sewage and pesticides and industrial contaminants that we are putting into it now, much less all that we will be capable of putting into it in a few years. We haven't accepted—we can't really believe—that the most characteristic product of our age of scientific miracles is junk, but that is so. And we still think and behave as though we face an unspoiled continent, with thousands of acres of living space for every man. We still sing "America the Beautiful" as though we had not created in it, by strenuous effort, at great expense, and with dauntless self-praise, an unprecedented ugliness.

The last couple of miles of our trip we could hear

off in the bottoms alongside us the cries of pileated woodpeckers, and we welcomed the news of them. These belong to the big trees and big woods, and more than any other birds along this river they speak out of our past. Their voices are loud and wild, the cries building strongly and then trailing off arhythmically and hesitantly as though reluctant to end. Though they never seemed very near, we could hear them clearly over the commotion of the water. There were probably only a pair or two of them, but their voices kept coming to us a long time, creating beyond the present wildness of the river, muddy from the ruin of mountainsides and farmlands, the intimation of another wildness that will not overflow again in *our* history.

The wind had finally made its way into our clothes, and our feet and hands and faces were beginning to stiffen a little with the cold. And so when home came back in sight we thought it wasn't too soon. We began to slant across the currents toward the shore. The river didn't stop to let us off. We ran the bow out onto the path that goes up to my house, and the current rippled on past the stern as though it were no more than the end of a stranded log. We were out of it, wobbling stiff-legged along the midrib on our way to the high ground.

With the uproar of the water still in our ears, we had as we entered the house the sense of having been utterly outside the lives we live as usual. My warm living room was a place we seemed to have been away from a long way. It needed getting used to.

THE LONG-LEGGED HOUSE

I

Sometime in the twenties, nobody knows exactly when any more, Curran Mathews built a cabin of two small rooms near Port Royal between the Kentucky River and the road, on a narrow strip of land belonging to my mother's father. Curran Mathews was my grandmother's bachelor brother. He died of cancer when I was a child and I have come to know him better since his death than I did while he was alive. At the time he died I knew him mostly as a sort of wanderer visiting in the family households, an inspired tinkerer with broken gadgetry and furniture, a man of small disciplines and solutions without either a home or a profession, and a teller of wonderful bedtime stories.

At that time the family still owned the building in Port Royal in which James Mathews, my great-grandfather, an immigrant from Ireland, had made shoes and run an undertaking business. There was a little partitioned-off space at the back of this building that Curran used as a workshop. He was good with tools, and a thorough workman—though I don't believe he ever made any money in that way, or ever intended to. I loved that little shop, and the smells of it, and spent some happy hours there. It smelled of varnish, and was filled with tools and objects of mysterious use. It was tucked away there, as if secretly, out of the way of the main coming and going of the town, looking out across the back lots into a pasture. And everything about it

110

partook of the excitement I felt in this man, home from his wanderings, with his precise ways and peculiarly concentrated silences. I sat in the open doorway there one afternoon, a rich plot of sunlight on the floor around me, Curran quietly at work in the room at my back; I looked up at the ridge beyond the town, the open, still sunlit country of the summer afternoon, and felt a happiness I will never forget.

As for the bedtime stories, they were inexhaustible and always lasted a fine long while past bedtime. He was a reader of adventure stories, and a deeply restless man who spent a large part of his life in distant places. And his stories fed on his reading and on his travels. They could keep going night after night for weeks, and then he would go off someplace. By the time he got back he would have "forgot" the story, and we would have to tell it to him up to where he left off, and then after grunting a little with effort he would produce the next installment. Some of these were straight out of books—I discovered later that he had told us, almost page by page, the first of the *Tarzan* stories; and some were adapted from Zane Grey. But others are harder to account for. I remember that the best one was a sort of Swiftian yarn about a boy who was kidnaped by the fairies, and escaped, and was captured and then adopted by a tribe of Indians, and escaped, and so on and on through a summer in which bedtime was, for a change, looked forward to.

He had a family side, and another side. The family side I knew, I suppose, well enough. The other side I still pick up the hearsay of in conversations here and there. The other side is wild, extravagant, funny in the telling, and for me always more than a little troubling and sad. There was something he needed that he never found. That other side of his life he lived alone. Though some of his doings are legendary among people who remember him, I believe he kept quiet about them himself, and I think I will do the same.

He built the cabin on the river because he thought it would improve his health to live more in the open. His health had never been good. He had permanently injured his leg in a buggy accident in his youth—he disguised his limp so well that he was taken into the army during World War I. And there seems reason to think that the disease that finally killed him had begun years back in his life.

But health must have been only the ostensible reason; the best reason for the cabin he built here must be that it was in his nature to have a house in the woods and to return now and again to live in it. For there was something deep about him, something quiet-loving and solitary and kin to the river and the woods. My mother remembers summer evenings in her girlhood when they would drive his old car five or six miles out in the country to a railroad section pond, where as it grew dark they would sit and listen for a certain bullfrog to croak—and when the frog croaked at last they would drive back to Port Royal. He did that, of course, partly for the entertainment of his young niece; but partly, too, he was entertaining himself. Given the same niece and the same need for entertainment, another man would not have thought of that. It must have been meaningful to him—a sort of ritual observance. Hard as it may be to know the needs and feelings of a man who said little about himself, dead now more than twenty years, that jaunting to hear the bullfrog does suggest how far his life escaped the categories. It was a life a man could hardly have carried in his wallet, or joined comfortably to the usual organizations.

And so his building of the cabin on the riverbank had a certain logic. The state road had not yet been built up the river on our side—that would have to wait for the Depression and the W.P.A. There was only a sort of rocked wagon-track going up through the bottoms, winding around the heads of slew-hollows, fording the creeks; farm fences crossed it, and one could not travel it without opening and closing gates. Only a few hundred yards down the river from the site of the cabin was Lane's Landing, the port of Port Royal, with its coal tipple and general store, but even so Curran Mathew's wooded stretch of riverbank was far more remote and isolated then than it is now. The voices of the frogs were here—there must have been summer nights when he sat awake a long time, listening to them. And there were other wild voices, too, that I know he heard, because I have heard them here myself. Through a notch in the far bank a little stream poured into the river, a clear moist sound, a part of the constancy of the place. And up in the thickets on the hillside there would be a cowbell, pastoral music, *tinkle-tink tink tink tinkle,* a sort of rhythmless rhythm late into the night sometimes, and nearby, when all else would be still. It was a place where a man, staying by himself, could become deeply quiet. It would have been a quiet that grew deeper and wider as the days passed, and would have come to include many things, both familiar and unexpected. If the stories about him are correct, and they doubtless are, Curran Mathews was not always alone here, and not always quiet. But there were times when he was both. He is said to have owned an old fiddle that he played at these times.

He did most of the building himself. And I imagine that those were days of high excitement. Except for the floors and the one partition, the lumber came out of an old log house that was built up on the hilltop by my grandfather's great-grandfather, Ben Perry. It surely must have been one of the first houses built in this part of the country. In my childhood the main part of it was still standing, and was known then as the Aunt Molly Perry House, after the last member of the family to live in it. It was in bad shape when I knew it, and hogs were being fed in it. Now there is nothing left but the stones of the chimneys piled up, and the well. The lot where it stood is still known, though, as the Old House

Lot, and it is a lovely place, looking out over the woods into the river valley. Some of the old locusts that stood in the yard are still there, and in the spring the little white starry flowers of old time dooryards still bloom in the grass. It is a place I like, and like to go to and sit down. I am not oppressed by it as I would be by an ancient and venerated family seat, full of old records and traditions and memories. I figure a ponderous amount of my historical inheritance took place there— it is one of the main routes on my way here—but none of it was written down, and most of it has been forgotten, and the house itself is gone. Last summer for a while I pastured a mare and colt up there in the Old House Lot, and where my forebears had sat down to meals three times a day for generations, the horses grazed and thought nothing of it, it being only daylight and grass to them. I sat sometimes on the piled stones of the old chimneys, watching them graze, and it seemed to me that my line had issued out of the ground there like a spring, as regardless of itself, in the historical sense anyhow, and as little able to memorialize itself, as water—and had trickled off into oblivion, as I said to myself that I would too, leaving the hill there looking into the valley, and the horses grazing in the sunlight. And I was more grateful for the silence of their departure than I would be for the lineage of a king. Not knowing who had planted the flowers there, I did not have to weep over them, or grow reminiscent, but could enjoy them as they were. I had them free as wildflowers.

But the house—or, anyhow, part of it—had a very pleasing resurrection. I think of Curran Mathews coming there one summer morning, full of the excitement of his vision of a cabin on the riverbank, to begin work. I can see him carefully prizing off the boards of the kitchen L—broad poplar and walnut boards cut to irregular thicknesses in some crude sawmill; and fine handmade tongue-and-groove paneling out of, I think, the dining room. The nails would probably have rusted tight in their holes, and it would have been slow, nagging work, getting boards off without splitting them, but Curran was a man capable of great persistence and patience when he wanted to be, and he got it done, and drew out the old hand-forged square-headed nails, and loaded his lumber, and hauled it down the hill to the riverbank where he intended to settle a new place. Figuring backward from my own experiences here later, I think I partly know what was on his mind then. He was striking out beyond the bounds of the accepted, beyond the ordinary and common things that most people respect—as any man does who sets a willing foot into the woods—and there would have been an exhilaration in that. As soon as he marked out the dimensions of his house on the ground the place would have begun to look different to him, would have begun to have an intimacy for him that it could never have had before. Earlier, any place he stood was more or less equal to any other place he stood; he would move on to another place. But once those boundaries were marked on the ground, there would have begun to be a permanent allegiance. Here was the tree that would stand by the door. This limb would reach across the porch. Looking out here would give a fine view of the water. Here was where the steppingstones must come down the slope. When he began clearing the ground he was an eager man, and he felt an eagerness that is felt only by men who are doing what they want passionately to do, and who are not justifying it in an account book. All this I have experienced myself, much of it in the same place and in the same way that he experienced it, and I know it must be so. But there is a great deal, too, that I don't know, and never will. What did he think in the nights he spent here alone? What desires and dreams came to him in his solitudes? Had he read Thoreau, I wonder— or any of the other writers and poets who have so shaped my life? I doubt it, and feel in that a large difference between us.

He built a cabin of two rooms, a bedroom and a kitchen. The bedroom opened onto a small screened porch, and an open porch went the rest of the way across the front and along the upriver side, railed with locust poles. He painted it with a green paint that in my time took on a bluish cast, weathered and natural-looking, a color unlike any I ever saw. It has somehow come to be associated in my mind with the lichens that grow here on the trunks of the trees, but it was more vivid. He planted a few shrubs around it, some of which are still living: two spiraeas and a bush honeysuckle whose translucent red berries I remember wanting badly to eat when I was a child. Though I could eat them now if I wanted to, I never have, certain they would taste worse than they look.

A few years ago I was given an old dim photograph of Curran from back in the days when he lived actively here on the river. It shows him at the top of a flight of steps he had just finished digging into the steep bank below the cabin. He is bent slightly forward, holding a shovel in his hands, looking up the slope. He is wearing an old limber-brimmed felt hat. You can barely see his face. Behind him his new steps go down to the river, where, under the lacy top of an overhanging willow, a boat rests lightly on the water.

I have no memory of the cabin as it stood on its original site. Before I was three years old, the flood of 1937 picked it up from where Curran had built it and carried it several feet downriver and up the bank, where it lodged against some trees, and was then anchored and given new underpinnings. But I knew it early, and my first memories of it, trivial as they are, involve a delight that I associate with no other place. The cabin had come to be known simply as the Camp—or, when one wanted to be very specific, Curran's Camp. Throughout my childhood "going down to the Camp" was to be going to the most exciting place. In my very early years it was often used as a family gathering place in the summers. We children had an Uncle Herbert who got to be known as Uncle River because we hardly ever saw him except at the Camp. And I had another uncle, Uncle Doc, with whom it was a ritual for me to go down the long flight of stone steps to the river to watch for boats—which usually never appeared, but whose mere possibility was charming enough. And I remember being put to bed there for a nap on the promise that when I woke up I could have a dish of chocolate pudding. I needed to be bribed, of course, for I knew even then that those were indispensable times. And Clio, the bitter Muse, has had her way even with that, for I remember the nap but have forgot the pudding.

Throughout my childhood there were trips to the Camp—some memorable, some forgotten. Those visits put the place deeply into my mind. It was a place I often thought about. I located a lot of my imaginings in it. Very early, I think, I began to be bound to the place in a relation so rich and profound as to seem almost mystical, as though I knew it before birth and was born for it. It remained so attractive to me, for one reason, because I had no bad associations with it. It was the family's wilderness place, and lay beyond the claims and disciplines and obligations that motivated my grownups. From the first I must have associated it with freedom. And I associated it with Curran, who must have associated it with freedom. It always had for me something of the charming strangeness of that man's life, as though he had carried it with him in his travels out in the West—as indeed I know he had, in his mind. Like Curran's life, the Camp seemed open to experiences not comprehended in the regularities of the other grown people. That is only to suggest the intensity and the nature of the bond; such feelings, coming from so far back in childhood, lie deeper than the reasons that are thought of afterward. But given the bond, it was no doubt inevitable that I would sooner or later turn to the place on my own, without the company of the grownups.

The first such visit I remember was during the flood of March, 1945. With my brother and a friend, I slipped away one bright Saturday and hitchhiked to Port Royal. We walked down to the Camp from there. It is one of the clearest days I have in my memory. The water was up over the floor of the Camp, and we spent a good while there, straddling out along the porch railings over the water—a dangerous business, of course, but we were in danger the rest of that day. There is something about a flooded house that is endlessly fascinating. Mystery again. One world being supplanted by another. But to a boy on a bright spring day it is without horror. I remember well the fascination I felt that day: the river pouring by, bright in the sun, laced with the complex shadows of the still naked trees, its currents passing the porch posts in little whirlpools the size of half dollars. The world suddenly looked profoundly alive and full of new interest. I had a transfiguring sense of adventure. The world lay before me, and Saturday lay before the world.

We left the Camp after a while and walked on up the river to where several johnboats were tied, and helped ourselves to the biggest one, a white one, built long and wide and heavy, as a boat must be when it is used for net fishing. We unfastened its mooring chain and pushed off. For oars we had an oak board about four feet long and an old broom worn off up to the bindings, but that seemed the paltriest of facts. We were free on the big water. Once we broke with the shore and disappeared into the bushes along the backwater, we were farther beyond the reach of our parents than we had ever been, and we knew it—and if our parents had known it, what a dark day it would have been for them! But they didn't. They were twelve miles away in New Castle, their minds on other things, assuming maybe that we had just gone to somebody's house to play basketball. And we had the world to ourselves—it would be years before we would realize how far we were from knowing what to do with it. That clumsy boat and our paddles seemed as miraculous as if we were cave men paddling the first dugout.

We paddled up to the Cane Run bridge and found the water over the road. Another wonder! And since it was unthinkable to refuse such an opportunity, we boated over the top of the road and entered the creek valley. We worked our way up through the treetops for some way, and broke out into a beautiful lake of the backwater, the sun on it and all around it the flooded woods. It was deeply quiet—nobody around anywhere, and nobody likely to be. The world expanded yet again. It would have taken an airplane to find us. From being mere boys—nine, ten, and eleven years old, I believe—we were enlarged beyond our dreams.

We went up the long backwater and into the woods. The woods is still there and I often go there these days to walk or to sit and look. It is a large stand of trees, and there is some big timber in it. I know it well now, but then I had only been there a few times to gather ferns with the rest of the family, and it was still new to me. The woods stands on a series of narrow low ridges divided by deep hollows. On the day of our adventure the backwater was in all these hollows, and we could go far into the woods without ever setting foot on the ground. That was another wondrous opportunity, and the hollows were numerous and long, allowing for endless variation and elaboration. The first wildflowers were blooming among the dead leaves above the water line, and I remember how green and suggestive the pads of moss looked in the warm water light, that time of the year. I gathered some and wrapped it in my handkerchief and put it in the boat, as if to take that place and the day with me when I left. We found a groundhog basking on a point of land, and got out and gave chase, thinking we had him cornered, only to see him take to the water and swim away. It never had occurred to me that groundhogs could swim, and I felt like a naturalist because of the discovery.

But it had to end, and it ended hard. When we started back the wind had risen, and drove strong against our boat. Our crude paddles lost their gleeful aura of makeshift, and turned against us. We moved like the hands of a clock, and only by the greatest effort. I don't think it occurred to any of us to worry about getting out, or even about being late, but being thwarted that way, pitted so against the wind and the water, had terror in it. Before we got safely back it had become a considerable ordeal—which, as soon as we *were* safely back, began to look like the best adventure of all. We tied the boat and walked up to the road, feeling like Conquerors, weary as Conquerors.

And there my grandparents were, waiting anxiously for us. We had been spied upon, it turned out. We had been seen taking the boat. Phone calls had been made. And my grandparents had driven down—in great fear, I'm sure—to see what was to be done. When we finally came off the river they were ready to give us up for drowned. They told us that. And suddenly we felt a good deal relieved to know we weren't.

That was the second bad flood to hit the Camp. These were modern floods, and man-made. Too many of the mountain slopes along the headwater streams had been denuded by thoughtless lumbering and thoughtless farming. Too little humus remained in the soil to hold the rains. After this second flood more of the old houses built near the river in earlier times would be abandoned. And in that spring of 1945 the war was about to end. Before long the country, as never before, would be full of people with money to spend. Men's demands upon nature were about to begin an amazing increase that would continue until now. The era when Curran Mathews conceived and built the Camp was coming to an end.

And two springs later Curran lay dying in the town of Carrollton at the mouth of the river. He had gone to spend his last days in the home of two of my aunts. From his bedroom in Carrollton the windows looked out across back yards and gardens toward the bluff over the valley of the Ohio. He couldn't see the river, but as always in a river town it would have been present to his mind, part of his sense of the place, the condition of everything else. The valley of the river that had been home to him all his life, and where his cabin stood in its woods patch on the bank, lay across town, behind him. He knew he wouldn't see it again.

That spring he watched the lengthening of the buds and the leafing out of a young beech near his window. And after the leaves had come he continued to watch it—the lights and moods and movements of it. He spoke often to my aunts of its beauty. I learned of this only a year or so ago. It has made his illness and death real to me, as they never were before. It has become one of the most vivid links in my kinship with him. How joyous the young tree must have been to him, who could have had so little joy then in himself. That he watched it and did not turn away from it must mean that he found joy in it, affirmed the life in it, even though his own life was painfully going out.

In those years of the war and of Curran's illness the Camp fell into disuse and neglect. The screens rotted; leaves piled up on the porch, and the boards decayed under them; the weeds and bushes grew up around it; window glasses were broken out by rock-throwers; drunks and lovers slipped in and out through the windows. And then one evening in early summer—it must have been the year after Curran's death, when I was nearly fourteen—I came down by myself just before dark, and cooked a supper on the riverbank below the house, and spent the night in a sleeping bag on the porch. I don't remember much about that night, and don't remember at all what reason I had for coming. But that night began a conscious relation between me and the Camp, and it has been in my mind and figured in my plans ever since.

I must have come, that first time, intending to stay for a while, though I can't remember how long. The next morning as I was finishing breakfast a car pulled in off the road and an old man got out, saying he had come to fish. Did I mind? Maybe I felt flattered that my permission had been asked. No, I didn't mind, I said. In fact, I'd fish with him. He was a friendly white-haired old man, very fat, smiling, full of talk. Would he like to fish from a boat? I asked him. I'd go get one. He said that would be fine, and I went down along the bank to the landing and got one—again, I think, by the forthright method of "borrowing"—and brought it back. It was a good big boat, but I had managed to find only a broken oar to paddle with. He got in with his equipment and we set off. We fished the whole day together. Not much was said. I don't remember that we ever introduced ourselves. But it was a friendly day. I was slow in moving us between fishing spots with my broken oar and I remember how he sat in the middle seat and hunched us along like a kid in a toy car. It helped a great deal. We fished until the late afternoon and caught—or, rather, *he* caught—a sizable string of little perch and catfish. When he left he gave me all the catch. He fished, he said, for the love of it. I don't yet know who he was. I never saw him again. In the evening, after I had taken the boat home and had started cleaning the fish on the porch, my friend Pete stopped by with his father. They had been working on their farm up the river that day, and were on their way home. Pete liked the look of things and decided to stay on with me. And that began a partnership that lasted a long time. The next morning we began scraping out the dried mud that the last high water had deposited on the floors—and suddenly the place entered our imagination. We quit being campers and became settlers. Twenty or so years before, the same meta-morphosis must have taken place in the mind of Curran Mathews. A dozen or two strokes, flaking up the sedi-ment from the floor—and we had got an idea, and been transformed by it: we'd clean her out and fix her up.

And that is what we did. We gave it a cleaning, and then scrounged enough furnishings and food from our families to set up in free and independent bachelorhood on the river. Pete's family had a well-stocked frozen-food locker that we acquired a deep respect for. The idea was to be well enough supplied that we wouldn't need to go back home for a while. That way, if somebody wanted to impose work or church on us they would have to come get us. That was another realization the Camp had suddenly lit up for us: We were against civilization, and wanted as little to do with it as possible. On the river we came aware of a most inviting silence: the absence of somebody telling us what to do and what not to do. We swam and fished and ate and slept. We could leave our clothes in the cabin and run naked down the bank and into the water. We could buy cigars and lie around and smoke. We could go out on the porch in the bright damp shadowy mornings and pee over the railing. We made a ritual of dispensing with nonessentials; one of us would wash the dishes with his shirttail, and the other would dry them with his. We were proud of that, and thought it had style.

For several years we came to the Camp every chance we got, and made good memories for ourselves. We will never live days like those again, and will never live happier ones. I suppose it was growing up that put an end to them—college, jobs, marriages and families of our own. We began to have a stake in civilization, and could no longer just turn our backs on it and go off. Back in our free days we used to tell people—a good deal to their delight, for we were both sons of respected lawyers—that we intended to be bootleggers. I think the foreknowledge of our fate lay in that. For to contrive long to be as free and careless as we were in those days we would have had to become bootleggers, or something of the kind. Ambition and responsibility would take us a different way.

During those years when I would come down to the Camp with Pete, I would also fairly often come alone. Pete, who was older than I was, would be having a date. Or he would have to stay home and work at a time when I could get free. And at times I came alone because I wanted to. I was melancholic and rebellious, and these moods would often send me off to the river.

Those times were quiet and lonely, troubled often by the vague uneasiness and dissatisfaction of growing up. The years I spent between childhood and manhood seem as strange to me now as they did then. Clumsy in body and mind, I knew no place I could go to and feel certain I ought to be there. I had no very good understanding of what I was rebelling against: I was going mostly by my feelings, and so I was rarely calm. And I didn't know with enough certainty what I wanted to be purposeful about getting it. The Camp offered no escape from these troubles, but it did allow them the dignity of solitude. And there were days there, as in no other place, when as if by accident, beyond any reason I might have had, I was deeply at peace, and happy. And those days that gave me peace suggested to me the possibility of a greater, more substantial peace—a decent, open, generous relation between a man's life and the world—that I have never achieved; but it must have begun to be then, and it has come more and more consciously to be, the hope and the ruling idea of my life.

I remember one afternoon when I tied my boat to a snag in the middle of the river outside the mouth of Cane Run, and began fishing. It was a warm sunny afternoon, quiet all around, and I had the river to myself. There is some nearly mystical charm about a boat that I have always been keenly aware of, and tied there that afternoon in midstream, a sort of island, it made me intensely alive to the charm of it. It seemed so intact and dry in its boatness, and I so coherent and satisfied in my humanness. I fished and was happy for sometime, until I became *conscious* of what a fine thing I was doing. It came to me that this was one of the grand possibilities of my life. And suddenly I became deeply uneasy, even distressed. What I had been at ease with, in fact and without thinking, had become, as a possibility, too large. I hadn't the thoughts for it. I hadn't the background for it. My cultural inheritance had prepared me to exert myself, work, move, "get someplace." To be idle, simply to live there in the sunlight in the middle of the river, was something I was not prepared to do deliberately. I tried to stay on, forcing myself to do what I now *thought* I ought to be doing, but the spell was broken. That I had nothing to do but what I wanted to do, and what I was in fact doing, had become utterly impotent as an idea. I had to leave. I would have to live to twice that age before I could do consciously what I wanted so much then to do. And even now I can do it only occasionally.

I read a good deal during those stays I made at the river. I read *Walden* here then—though I can't remember whether it was for the first or second time. And I was beginning to read poetry with some awareness that it interested me and was important to me—an awareness I had not yet come by in any classroom. I had a paperback anthology of English and American poems, and I would lie in bed at night and read it by the light of a kerosene lamp. One night I lay there late and read for the first time and was deeply stirred by Gray's "Elegy Written in a Country Churchyard." It seemed to me to be a fine thing, and I thought I understood it and knew why it was fine. That was a revealing experience. While I read a dog was howling somewhere down the river, and an owl was calling over in the Owen County bottom, and my father's old nickel-plated Smith and Wesson revolver lay in the bedding under my head. I loved this place and had begun to understand it a little—but I didn't love it and understand it well enough yet to be able to trust it in the dark. That revolver belonged on top of the bookcase at home, but nobody ever thought of it, and I could borrow it and bring it back without fear that it would be missed.

The Camp was not the only place that was important to me. But during the winters of those years, starting when I was fourteen, when I was away at school, it lay in my mind with the other places that were important, part of what I dreamed of coming home to. During the

years of high school, particularly, I believe that the
thought of it was indispensable to me. The school I
attended was a military school. There military correct-
ness and regularity were always the aim—thwarted
constantly, to be sure, by the natural high spirits of the
students and by the natural mediocrity of most of the
teachers—but when thwarted always exacting vengeance
on somebody. Sympathy and intelligence were in everything replaced by rules, and by a long ago outworn—
hence, threatened and fanatical—moral dogmatism. The
highest aim of the school was to produce a perfectly
obedient, militarist, puritanical moron who could play
football. That aim, of course, inspired a regime that was
wonderfully vindictive against anything that threatened
to be exceptional. And having a lively and independent
mind, I became a natural enemy of the regime. Take a
simpleton and give him power and confront him with
intelligence—and you have a tyrant. I was once struck
by one of the teachers for using a dictionary (not an
authorized textbook) during a study hall, and another
time was openly chastised for reading a story by Balzac
entitled "A Passion in the Desert," the only passion
authorized by the regime being a passionate servility.
The "discipline" exercised by the student officers was
often equally stupid, and often more violent. I waged
four years there in sustained rebellion against everything
the place stood for, paying the cost both necessarily and
willingly. I was not, during all those years, well equipped
for such a struggle—though I was a conscious student
of resistance, and got pretty good at it toward the end.
I had, maybe because of the prolonged awkwardness
of my adolescence, an enormous craving for personal
dignity—and in the military school dignity simply was
not possible for one who was not an athlete and who
could not regard mechanical obedience as the summit
of virtue. I don't think I could have survived that struggle intact if I hadn't had a history that taught me that
there was dignity of another kind, and more desirable.
I had known from the beginning a few men who ac-

cepted and required of themselves as men with a great simplicity of pride, who could be lonely in their virtues and excellences if they had to be, and who could move in their lives without either crawling or marching—and the thought of those men was before me. But also I had lived days of my own, perhaps mainly at the Camp, when my life had seemed to come to me naturally, with an ease and rightness, as life must come to the king-fishers on the river. I knew that these were my best days, and knew they had not come to me on the orders of anybody or because of anybody's opinion of them or because somebody had allowed me to have them. I knew they were my holy days, my sabbaths, and they had come to me freely because I was free. Knowing that, I knew that men were most admirable singly, and that standing in lines under the command of other men is the least becoming thing they do. Though I stood in line many times each day, my privilege was that my mind was *not* in line. It didn't *have* to be. It had better places to go. Now that I think of it, I had, by that time, a superbly furnished mind. It was not yet much furn-ished with books, for I had not read many books, or many good ones, then; it was furnished with the knowl-edge of a few good men and good places and good days that had come to me in my life. I was not servile because I knew what it was *not* to be servile. It is bound to be in some sense true that a man is not a slave if his mind is free. It is the man who can think of no alternative to his enslavement who is truly a slave. Though I found the life at the military school to be often painful and interminably hateful, I was coherent and steadfast in my rebellion against it because I knew, I *must* have known, that I was the creature of another place, and that my life was already given to another way.

What I remember best from those years are the days in early summer when I would first come down to the Camp to clean the place up. By the time school would be out the weeds there on the damp riverbank would

have already grown waist-high. I would come down
with ax and scythe, preparatory to some stay I intended
to make, and drive back the wilderness. I would mow
the wild grass and horseweeds and nettles and elder-
berries, and chop down the tree sprouts, and trim ob-
structive branches off the nearby trees. It would be hard
to describe the satisfaction this opening up would give
me. I would sit down now and again to rest and dry the
sweat a little, and look at what I had done. I would
meditate on the difference I had made, and my mind
would be full of delight. It was some instinctive love of
wildness that would always bring me back here, but it
was by the instincts of a farmer that I established myself. The Camp itself was not imaginable until the weeds
were cut around it; until that was done I could hardly
bring myself to enter it. A house is not simply a building, it is also an enactment. That is the first law of
domesticity, even the most meager. The mere fact must
somehow be turned into meaning. Necessity must be
made a little ceremonious. To ever arrive at what one
would call home even for a few days, a decent, thoughtful approach must be made, a clarity, an opening.

Only after I had mowed and trimmed around it, so
that it stood clear of its surroundings, or clearly within
them, could I turn to the house. The winter's leaves
would have to be swept off the porch, the doors opened,
the shutters opened, daylight filling the rooms for the
first time in months, the sashes drawn back in their
slots, the walls and floors swept. And then, finished,
having earned the right to be there again, I would go
out on the porch and sit down. Tired and sweaty, the
dust of my sweeping still flavoring the air, I would have
a wonderful sense of order and freedom. The old
recognitions would come back, the familiar sights and
sounds slowly returning to their places in my mind. It
would seem inexpressibly fine to be living, a joy to
breathe.

During the last of my college years and the year I
spent as a graduate student, the Camp went through an-

other period of neglect. There were distractions. I had begun to be preoccupied with the girl I was going to marry. In a blundering, half-aware fashion I was becoming a writer. And, as I think of it now, school itself was a distraction. Although I have become, among other things, a teacher, I am skeptical of education. It seems to me a most doubtful process, and I think the good of it is taken too much for granted. It is a matter that is overtheorized and overvalued and always approached with too much confidence. It is, as we skeptics are always discovering to our delight, no substitute for experience or life or virtue or devotion. As it is handed out by the schools, it is only theoretically useful, like a randomly mixed handful of seeds carried in one's pocket. When one carries them back to one's own place in the world and plants them, some will prove unfit for the climate or the ground, some are sterile, some are not seeds at all but little clods and bits of gravel. Surprisingly few of them come to anything. There is an incredible waste and clumsiness in most efforts to prepare the young. For me, as a student and as a teacher, there has always been a pressing anxiety between the classroom and the world: how can you get from one to the other except by a blind jump? School is not so pleasant or valuable an experience as it is made out to be in the theorizing and reminiscing of elders. In a sense, it is not an experience at all, but a hiatus in experience.

My student career was over in the spring of 1957, and I was glad enough to be done with it. My wife and I were married in May of that year. In the fall I was to take my first teaching job. We decided to stay through the summer at the Camp. For me, that was a happy return. For Tanya, who was hardly a country girl, it was a new kind of place, confronting her with hardships she could not have expected. We were starting a long way from the all-electric marriage that the average modern American girl supposedly takes for granted. If Tanya had been the average modern American girl, she would probably have returned me to bachelorhood within a week—but then, of course, she would have had no interest in such a life, or in such a marriage, in the first place. As it was, she came as a stranger into the country where I had spent my life, and made me feel more free and comfortable in it than I had ever felt before. That seems to me the most graceful generosity that I know.

For weeks before the wedding I spent every spare minute at the Camp, getting it ready to live in. I mowed around it, and cleaned it out, and patched the roof. I replaced the broken windowpanes, and put on new screens, and whitewashed the walls, and scrounged furniture out of various family attics and back rooms. As a special wedding gift to Tanya I built a new privy— which never aspired so high as to have a door, but did sport a real toilet seat.

All this, I think, was more meaningful and proper than I knew at the time. To a greater extent than is now common, or even possible for most men, I had by my own doing prepared the house I was to bring my wife to, and in preparing the house I prepared myself. This was the place that was more my own than any other in the world. In it, I had made of loneliness a good thing. I had lived days and days of solitary happiness there. And now I changed it, to make it the place of my marriage. A complex love went into those preparations —for Tanya, and for the place too. Working through those bright May days, the foliage fresh and full around me, the river running swift and high after rain, was an act of realization: as I worked, getting ready for the time when Tanya would come to live there with me, I understood more and more what the possible meanings were. If it had gone differently—if it had followed, say, the prescription of caution: first "enough" money, and then the "right" sort of house in the "right" sort of place—I think I would have been a poorer husband. And my life, I know, would have been poorer. It wasn't, to be sure, a permanent place that I had prepared; we were going to be there only for the one summer. It was, maybe one ought to say, no more than a ritual. But it was a meaningful and useful ritual.

That is more than I am able to say of our wedding. Our wedding reminds me a little of the Kentucky Derby; the main event, which lasted only a couple of minutes, required days of frantic prologue. During this commotion one must discontinue one's own life and attempt to emulate everybody. Nobody can be still until convinced that this marriage will be like everybody else's. The men insinuate. The women gloat. The church is resurrected and permitted to interfere. As at funerals, the principals cannot be decently let alone, but must be overhauled, upgraded, and messed with until they are not recognizable. During the week up to and including the wedding I am sure I was at the center of more absurdity than I hope ever to be at the center of again. One of my unforgettable moments, as they are called, was a quaint session with the minister who having met me for the first time that moment, and being scarcely better acquainted with Tanya, undertook to instruct us in the marital intimacies. A display of preacherish cant and presumption unusual even for a preacher, and all carried out with a slogging joyless dutifulness. As we were leaving he handed us a book on marriage. In a country less abject before "expert advice," the effrontery of it would be incredible. Well, be damned to him and his book, too. We thrive in spite of him, and in defiance of some of his rules. We are, I like to think, his Waterloo —though I know that, like most of his kind, he had come to his Waterloo before that, and survived by his inability to recognize it.

In any sense that is meaningful, our wedding was made in our marriage. It did not begin until the ceremony was over. It began, it seems to me, the next morning when we went together to the Camp for the first time since I started work on it. I hesitate to try to represent here the pleasure Tanya may have felt on this first arrival at our house, or the pride that I felt—those feelings were innocent enough, and probably had no more foundation than innocence needs. The point is that, for us, these feelings were substantiated by the Camp; they had its atmosphere and flavor, and partook of its history. That morning when Tanya first came to it as my wife, its long involvement in my life was transformed, given a richness and significance it had not had before. It had come to a suddenly illuminating promise. A new life had been added to it, as a new life had been added to my life. The ramshackle old house and my renewal of it particularized a good deal more for us than we could have realized then. We began there. It began that morning to have as profound a significance in our marriage as it had already had in my life.

We carried in what we had brought in the way of baggage, and then went out and bought the kitchen utensils and groceries we needed. In that way we began our marriage. And in that way—which may be only to say the same thing—we outdistanced what the sterile formalities of the wedding had expected of us or prescribed to us. We escaped the dead hands of the conventions and the institutions into a life that was distinctly our own. Our marriage became then, and has remained, the center of our life. And it is peculiarly true that the Camp is at the center of our marriage, both as actuality and as symbol. The memories of that first summer are strong and clear, and they stay in our minds. After we left the Camp at the summer's end, we continued to think of it and to talk about it and to make plans for it. We lived in other places in Kentucky, in California, in Europe, in New York—and now we have come back to live in sight and in calling distance of the place where we began. It is our source and our emblem, and it keeps its hold.

It would be a mistake to imply that two lives can unite and make a life between them without discord and pain. Marriage is a perilous and fearful effort, it seems to me. There can't be enough knowledge at the beginning. It must endure the blundering of ignorance. It is both the cause and the effect of what happens to it. It creates pain that it is the only cure for. It is the only comfort for its hardships. In a time when divorce is as accepted and conventionalized as marriage, a marriage that lasts must look a little like a miracle. That ours lasts—and in its own right and its own way, not in pathetic and hopeless parody of some "expert" notion— is largely, I believe, owing to the way it began, to the Camp and what it meant and came to mean. In coming there, we avoided either suspending ourselves in some honeymoon resort or sinking ourselves into the stampede for "success." In the life we lived that summer we represented to ourselves what we wanted—and it was *not* the headlong pilgrimage after money and comfort and prestige. We were spared that stress from the beginning. And there at the Camp we had around us the elemental world of water and light and earth and air. We felt the presences of the wild creatures, the river, the trees, the stars. Though we had our troubles, we had them in a true perspective. The universe, as we could see any night, is unimaginably large, and mostly empty, and mostly dark. We knew we needed to be together more than we needed to be apart.

There were physical hardships, or what pass these days for physical hardships, that scandalized certain interested onlookers. How, they wondered, could I think of bringing a girl like Tanya into a place like that? The question ought to have been: How could a girl like Tanya think of it? They will never know. We had no electricity, no plumbing, no new furniture. Our house would, no doubt, have been completely invisible to the average American bride and groom of that year, and when it rained hard enough the roof leaked. I think our marriage is better for it. By these so-called "hardships" —millions of people put up with much worse as a matter of course and endlessly—we freed our marriage of things. Like Thoreau at Walden, we found out what the essentials are. Our life will never be distorted by the feeling that there are luxuries we cannot do without. We will not have the anxiety of an abject dependence on gadgets and corporations. We are, we taught ourselves by our beginning, the dependents of each other, not of the local electric company.

That summer has no story; it has not simplified itself enough in my memory to have the consistency of a story and maybe it never will; the memories are too numerous and too diverse, and too deeply rooted in my life.

One of the first things I did after we got settled was to put some trotlines in the river—an early outbreak of male behavior that Tanya, I think, found both mystifying and depraved. On a dark rainy night in early June we had stayed up until nearly midnight, making strawberry preserves, and I decided on an impulse to go and raise my lines. Working my way along the line in pitch dark a few minutes later, I pulled out of the middle of the river a catfish that weighed twenty-seven pounds. Tanya had already gone to bed, and had to get up again to hear me congratulate myself in the presence of the captive. And so, indelibly associated with the early days of my marriage is a big catfish. Perhaps it is for the best.

The night of the Fourth of July of that year there came one of the worst storms this part of the country ever knew. For hours the rain spouted down on our tin roof in a wild crashing that did not let up. The Camp had no inner walls or ceilings; it was like trying to sleep inside a drum. The lightning strokes overlapped, so that it would seem to stay light for minutes at a stretch, and the thunder kept up a great knocking at the walls. After a while it began to seem unbelievable that the rain did not break through the roof. It was an apocalyptic night. The next morning we went out in bright sunshine to find the river risen to the top of its banks. There was a lasting astonishment in looking at it, and a sort of speculative fear; if that storm had reached much farther upstream we would have had to swim out of bed. Upstream, we could see several large trees that Cane Run had torn out by the roots and hurled clear

across the river to lodge against the Owen County bank.
The marks of that rain are still visible here.

And I remember a quiet night of a full moon when
we rowed the boat up into the bend above the mouth
of Cane Run, and let the slow current bring us down
again. I sat on the rower's seat in the middle of the
boat, and Tanya sat facing me in the stern. We stayed
quiet, aware of a deep quietness in the country around
us, the sky and the water and the Owen County hills
all still in the white stare of the moon. The wooded
hill above the Camp stood dark over us. As it bore us,
the current turned us as though in the slow spiral of a
dance.

Summer evenings here on the river have a quietness
and a feeling of completion about them that I have
never known in any other place, and I have kept in
mind the evenings of that summer. The wind dies about
sundown, and the surface of the river grows smooth.
The reflections of the trees lie inverted and perfect on
it. Occasionally a fish will jump, or a kingfisher hurry,
skreaking, along the fringe of willows. In the clearing
around the house the phoebes and pewees call from
their lookout perches, circling out and back in their
hunting flights as long as the light lasts. Out over the
water the swallows silently pass and return, dipping and
looping, climbing and dipping and looping, sometimes
skimming the surface to drink or bathe as they fly. The
air seems to come alive with the weaving of their paths.
As I sat there watching from the porch those evenings,
sometimes a profound peacefulness would come to me,
as it had at other times, but now it came of an awareness not only of the place, but of my marriage, a com-
pleteness I had not felt before. I was there not only
because I wanted to be, as always before, but now because Tanya was there too.

But most of all I like to remember the mornings. We
would get up early, and I would go out on the river to
raise my lines the first thing. There is no light like that
on the river on a clear early morning. It is fresh and

damp and full of glitters. The intense linear reflections off the wind waves wobble up the tree trunks and under the leaves. It was fishing that paid well, though not always in fish. When I came back to the Camp Tanya would have a big breakfast waiting.

After we ate I would carry a card table out into a corner of the little screened porch, and sit down to write. I would put in the morning there, conscious always as I worked of the life of the river. Fish would jump. A kingfisher would swing out over the water, blue and sudden in the water light, making his harsh ratcheting boast to startle the world. The green herons would pass intently up and down, low to the water, just outside the willows, like busy traffic. Or one would stop to fish from a snag or a low-bending willow, a little nucleus of stillness; sitting at my own work on the other side of the river I would feel an emanation of his intent silence; he was an example to me. And in the trees around the Camp all the smaller birds would be deep in their affairs. It might be that a towboat—the *Kentuckian* or the old *John J. Kelly*, that summer—would come up, pushing two bargeloads of sand to Frankfort. Or there would be somebody fishing from the other bank, or from a boat. And the river itself was as intricately and vigorously alive as anything on it or in it, always shifting its lights and its moods.

That confirmed me in one of my needs. I have never been able to work with any pleasure facing a wall, or in any other way fenced off from things. I need to be in the presence of the world. I need a window or a porch, or even the open outdoors. I have always had a lively sympathy for Thoreau's idea of a hypaethral book, a roofless book. Why should I shut myself up to write? Why not write and live at the same time?

There on the porch of the Camp that summer I wrote the first poetry that I still feel represented by—a long poem rather ostentatiously titled "Diagon," about the river—and did some of the most important reading I have ever done.

In the spring of that year I had read attentively
through the poems of Andrew Marvell, and had felt a
strong kinship with him. The poem of his that interested
me most was not one of the familar short poems, but
the strange, imperfect long one entitled "Upon Appleton
House, to my Lord *Fairfax.*" This is a complimentary
piece, evidently very deliberately undertaken, and in
long stretches it is amply boring. But in his description
of the countryside Marvell's imagination seems abruptly
to break out of the limitations of subject and genre, and
he wrote some stunning poetry. It has remained for me
one of the most exciting poems I know—not just in spite
of its faults, but to a considerable extent because of
them. I need to quote extensively from it, both to show
the quality of the best work in the poem and to show
what I think is remarkable about it. To begin with, all
this is most *particularly* observed—as rarely happens
in English nature poetry; the scene is of interest in itself,
not just as the manifestation of something transcendent
or subjective. The grass is grass, and one feels the real
rankness and tallness of it. Equally, the killed bird is
real; its blood is on the scythe's edge, and we feel the
mower's regret of the useless death. What natural
things manifest, if observed closely enough, is their
nature, and their nature is to change. Marvell's landscape is in constant metamorphosis, and so metaphor
is peculiarly necessary to its poetry—it is continuously
being carried beyond what it was. The comparative
image is not imposed from without by the poet, but is
seen by the poet to be implicit in the nature of the thing:
it is in the nature of a meadow to be like a sea.

> And how to the Abbyss I pass
> Of that unfathomable Grass,
> Where Men like Grashoppers appear,
> But Grashoppers are Gyants there:
> They, in their squeking Laugh, contemn
> Us as we walk more low then them:

And, from the Precipices tall
Of the green spir's, to us do call.

To see Men through this Meadow Dive,
We wonder how they rise alive.
As, under Water, none does know
Whether he fall through it or go.
But, as the Marriners that sound,
And show upon their Lead the Ground,
They bring up Flow'rs so to be seen,
And prove they've at the Bottom been.

No Scene that turns with Engines strange
Does oftner then these Meadows change.
For when the Sun the Grass hath vext,
The tawny Mowers enter next;
Who seem like *Israalites* to be,
Walking on foot through a green Sea.
To them the Grassy Deeps divide,
And crowd a Lane to either Side.

With whistling Sithe, and Elbow strong,
These Massacre the Grass along:
While one, unknowing, carves the *Rail*,
Whose yet unfeather'd Quils her fail.
The Edge all bloody from its Breast
He draws, and does his stroke detest . . .

          . . . .

The Mower now commands the Field;
In whose new Traverse seemeth wrougth
A Camp of Battail newly fought:
Where, as the Meads with Hay, the Plain
Lyes quilted ore with Bodies slain . . .

          . . . .

When after this 'tis pil'd in Cocks,
Like a calm Sea it shews the Rocks:
We wondring in the River near

How Boats among them safely steer.

. . . .

This *Scene* again withdrawing brings
A new and empty Face of things;
A levell'd space, as smooth and plain,
As Clothes for *Lilly* stretched to stain.
The World when first created sure
Was such a Table rase and pure.

. . . .

For to this naked equal Flat,
Which *Levellers* take Pattern at,
The Villagers in common chase
Their Cattle, which it closer rase . . .

. . . .

They feed so wide, so slowly move,
As *Constellations* do above.
Then, to conclude these pleasant Acts,
Denton sets ope its *Cataracts;*
And makes the Meadow truly be
(What it but seem'd before) a Sea.

. . . .

The River in it self is drown'd,
And Isl's th' astonished Cattle round.

Let others tell the *Paradox,*
How Eels now bellow in the Ox;
How Horses at their Tails do kick,
Turn'd as they hang to Leeches quick;
How Boats can over Bridges sail;
And Fishes do the Stables scale.
How *Salmons* trespassing are found;
And Pikes are taken in the Pound.

As I worked that summer I had these lines of Marvell
very fresh in my mind, and they were having a deeper

influence on me than I knew. My problem as a writer, though I didn't clearly know it yet, was that I had inherited a region that had as a literary tradition only the corrupt and crippling local colorism of the "Kentucky" writers. This was both a mythologizing chauvinism and a sort of literary imperialism, tirelessly exploiting the clichés of rural landscape, picking and singing and drinking and fighting lazy hillbillies, and Bluegrass Colonels. That is a blinding and tongue-tying inheritance for a young writer. And one doesn't even have to read the books to get it; it is so thoroughly established and accredited that it is propagated by schoolteachers, politicians, official bulletins, postcards, and the public at large. Kentucky is a sunny, beautiful land, full of happy country folks, whose very failures are quaint and delightful and to be found only here. It is surely no accident that along with this tradition of literary falsification there has been a tradition, equally well-established, and one could almost say equally respected, of political and industrial exploitation that has defaced and destroyed more of the state's beauty and wealth than there is left. The truth was too hard to tell; the language of the state's writers was dead in their mouths and they could not tell it. And when one finally told the clean truth, as Harry Caudill did in *Night Comes to the Cumberlands,* how few could hear it! And for the same reason. The people's ears are stuffed with the dead language of their literature. All my life as a writer I have had this rag bag of chauvinistic clichés to struggle with.

It is not difficult to see how serviceable and clarifying I found those lines from "Upon Appleton House." They showed me the poet's vision breaking out of its confines into the presence of its subject. I feel yet the exhilaration and release when Marvell turns from his elaborate overextended compliment to the noble family, and takes up a matter that really interested him; the full powers of his imagination and intelligence become suddenly useful to him, and necessary:

> And now the Abbyss I pass
> Of that unfathomable Grass. . . .

He is talking about a river valley of farms and wood-
lands such as I had known all my life, and now had
before me as I wrote and read through that summer.
As a child I had even believed, on what I then considered the best advice, in the metamorphosis of horse-
hairs that Marvell alludes to in the last stanza of his
description of the meadows. I would put hairs from tails
and manes into the watering trough at night, confident
that by morning they would be turned to snakes. But
I was a poor scientist, and in the mornings always forgot to look—and so kept the faith.

With Marvell's work in my mind, I began that summer of my marriage the surprisingly long and difficult
labor of *seeing* the country I had been born in and had
lived my life in until then. I think that this was peculiarly important and necessary to me; for whereas
most American writers—and even most Americans—of
my time are displaced persons, I am a placed person.
For longer than they remember, both sides of my family
have lived within five or six miles of this riverbank
where the old Camp stood and where I sit writing now.
And so my connection with this place comes not only
from the intimate familiarity that began in babyhood,
but also from the even more profound and mysterious
knowledge that is inherited, handed down in memories
and names and gestures and feelings, and in tones and
inflections of voice. I never, for reasons that could perhaps be explained, lost affection for this place, as
American writers have almost traditionally lost affection
for their rural birthplaces. I have loved this country
from the beginning, and I believe I was grown before I
ever really confronted the possibility that I could live
in another place. As a writer, then, I have had this place
as my fate. For me, it was never a question of *finding*
a subject, but rather of learning what to do with the
subject I had had from the beginning and could not

escape. Whereas most of this country's young writers
seem able to relate to no place at all, or to several, I
am related absolutely to one.

And this place I am related to not only shared the
state's noxious literary inheritance, but had, itself, never
had a writer of any kind. It was, from a writer's point
of view, undiscovered country. I have found this to be
both an opportunity and a disadvantage. The opportunity is obvious. The disadvantage is that of solitude.
Everything is to be done. No beginnings are ready-
made. One has no proof that the place can be written
about, no confidence that it can produce such a poet as
one suspects one might be, and there is a hesitance
about local names and places and histories because they
are so naked of associations and assigned values—none
of which difficulties would bother a poet beginning in
Concord, say, or the Lake District. But here I either
had to struggle with these problems or not write. I was
so intricately dependent on this place that I did not
begin in any meaningful sense to be a writer until I
began to see the place clearly and for what it was. For
me, the two have been the same.

That summer I was only beginning, and my poem
"Diagon" came out of the excitement of that first seeing, and the first inklings that there might be viable
meanings in what I knew. I was seeing consciously the
lights and colors and forms of my own world for the
first time:

> The sun sets vision afloat,
> Its hard glare down
> All the reaches of the river,
> Light on the wind waves
> Running to shore. Under the light
> River and hill divide. Two dead
> White trees stand in the water,
> The shimmering river casts
> A net of light around them,
> Their snagged shapes break through.

It is a descriptive poem mostly, and I have worried at times because in my work I have been so often preoccupied with description. But I have begun to think of that as necessary. I had to observe closely—be disciplined by the look and shape and feel of things and places—if I wanted to escape the blindness that would have made my work sound like an imitation of some Kentucky politician's imitation of the Romantic poets.

Sustaining and elaborating the effect of Marvell were the poems of William Carlos Williams, whose work I had known before but read extensively and studiously during that summer of 1957. I had two books of his, the *Collected Earlier Poems,* and his newest one, *Journey to Love.* I saw how his poems had grown out of his life in his native city in New Jersey, and his books set me free in my own life and my own place as no other books could have. I'll not forget the delight and hopefulness I felt in reading them. They relieved some of the pressure in the solitude I mentioned earlier. Reading them, I felt I had a predecessor, if not in Kentucky then in New Jersey, who confirmed and contemporized for me the experience of Thoreau in Concord.

Another book that deeply affected me that summer was Kenneth Rexroth's *100 Poems from the Chinese,* which immediately influenced my work and introduced me to Oriental poetry, not to mention the happy reading it made. I still think it is one of the loveliest books I know.

All these—my new marriage, the Camp, the river, the reading and writing—are intimately associated in my mind. It would be impossible to do more than imply the connections. Those were probably the three most important months in my life, as well as the happiest. When the summer was over it was a sharp sorrow to have to go. I remember us loading our borrowed household things into and onto our old Jeep station wagon and driving off up the river road on a brilliant day, the fields in the bottoms all yellow with the fall flowers.

And I remember the troubling sense that what we were going to would be more ordinary than what we were leaving behind. And it was.

II

It has been almost exactly a year since I began this history. My work was interrupted by the spring weather, when gardening and other outside concerns took me away from writing. But now it is deep winter again. Yesterday snow fell all day and covered the ground. This morning, though the sun came up clear, the thermometer read four above—a good morning to sit in the Camp in the warmth of the stove and the brisk snow light from the big window over the table. It is a morning for books and notebooks and the inviting blank pages of writing paper.

For people who live in the country there is a charming freedom in such days. One is free of obligations to the ground. There is no outside work that one ought to do, simply because, with the ground frozen deep and covered with snow, no such work is possible. Growth has stopped; there is plenty of hay and grain in the barn; the present has abated its urgencies. And the mind may again turn freely to the past and look back on the way it came. This morning has been bearing down out of the future toward this bit of riverbank forever. And for perhaps as long, in a sense, my life has been approaching from the opposite direction. The approach of a man's life out of the past is history, and the approach of time out of the future is mystery. Their meeting is the present, and it is consciousness, the only time life is alive. The endless wonder of this meeting is what causes the mind, in its inward liberty of a frozen morning, to turn back and question and remember. The world is full of places. Why is it that I am here?

What has interested me in telling the history of the Camp is the possibility of showing how a place and a person can come to belong to each other—or, rather, how a person can come to belong to a place, for places really belong to nobody. There is a startling reversal of our ordinary sense of things in the recognition that we are the belongings of the world, not its owners. The social convention of ownership must be qualified by this stern fact, and by the humility it implies, if we are not to be blinded altogether to where we are. We may deeply affect a place we own for good or ill, but our lives are nevertheless included in its life; it will survive us, bearing the results. Each of us is a part of a succession. I have come here following Curran Mathews. Who was here or what was done before he came, I do not know. I know that he had predecessors. It is certain that at some time the virgin timber that once stood here was cut down, and no doubt somebody then planted corn among the stumps, and so wore out the ground and allowed the trees to return. Before the white men were the Indians, who generation after generation bequeathed the country to their children, whole, as they received it. The history is largely conjecture. The future is mystery altogether: I do not know who will follow me. These realizations are both aesthetic and moral; they clear the eyes and prescribe an obligation.

At the point when my story was interrupted, my life no longer seemed to be bearing toward this place, but away from it. In the early fall of 1957 Tanya and I left the Camp, and through the following year I taught at Georgetown College. In the spring of 1958 our daughter Mary was born, and in the fall we left Kentucky for the West Coast. The Camp was closed and shuttered. Even though it had taken a new and lasting hold on my mind, it had entered another time of neglect. Three years would pass before I would come back to it. Toward the end of that summer of 1958 my friend Ed McClanahan and I made a canoe trip down the river and spent a night in the Camp, sleeping on the floor. For me, that night had the sadness of a parting. I was about to leave the state; the past was concluded, and the future, not yet begun, was hardly imaginable. The

Camp was empty, dark, full of finished memories, already falling back into the decay of human things that humans have abandoned. I was glad when the morning came, and we loafed on down along the shady margin of the river, watching the muskrats and the wood ducks.

I did not go back to the Camp again until the May of 1961. After two years on the West Coast, we had spent another year in Kentucky, this time on the farm, and again we had a departure ahead of us; late in the summer we would be going to Europe for a year. In order to prepare myself for this experience I began spending some mornings and rainy days at the Camp. My intention at first was to do some reading that would help me to understand the life of the places I would be seeing in Europe. But as I might have expected it was not Europe that most held my attention on those days, but the Camp and the riverbank and the river. It soon became clear that I was not so much preparing for an important experience as *having* an important one. I had been changed by what had happened to me and what I had learned during the last three years, and I was no sooner back at the Camp, with the familiar trees around me and the river in front of me again, than I began to see it differently and in some ways more clearly than I had before. Through that summer I wrote a sort of journal, keeping account of what I saw.

I first went back to the Camp that year on a rainy Monday, May 8. Heavy rains had begun the Saturday before, and the river was in flood. The water was under the house, within about a foot and a half of the floor. I had come to read, but mostly I sat and looked. How can one read history when the water is rising? The presence of the present had become insistent, undeniable, and I could not look away; the past had grown still, and could be observed at leisure in a less pressing time. The current was driving drift logs against the legs of the cabin beneath my chair. The river flexed and throbbed against the underpinnings like a great muscle, its vibrations too set in my nerves to permit thinking of anything else.

The river had become a lake, but a lake *flowing,* a continuous island of drift going down the channel, moving swiftly and steadily but forever twisting and eddying within itself; and along the edges the water was picking up little sticks and leaves and bits of grass as it rose. The house's perspective on the river had become the same as that of a boat. I kept an uneasy sense of its nearness, knowing that it was coming nearer; in an hour and a quarter it rose five inches. And there was a sort of permanent astonishment at its massiveness and flatness and oblivious implacable movement.

That day a new awareness of the Camp came to me, an awareness that has become a part of my understanding of all houses. It was a boat—a futile, ill-constructed, doomed boat—a boat such as a child might make on a hilltop. It had been built to stand there on the bank according to the rules of building on solid ground. But now the ground was under water, and the water was rising. The house would have the river to contend with. It would be called on to be a boat, as it had been called on before—as in the 1937 flood it had been called on, and had made its short voyage downstream and up the bank until it lodged among the trees. It was a boat by necessity, but not by nature, which is a recipe for failure. It was built with kinder hopes, to fare in a gentler element than water. All houses are not failed boats, but all are the failed, or failing, vehicles of some alien element; of wind, or fire, or time. When I left that night the river was only a foot beneath the floor, and still rising.

It rose two feet into the Camp, cresting sometime Wednesday. It was out of the house again by Thursday afternoon, and I opened the doors to dry the mud. On Sunday I was at work at a table on the screened porch, sitting in a chair where I could have sat in a boat a few days before, looking down into a landscape that still bore everywhere the marks of overflowing. As far as I

could see, up and down and across the valley, there was
the horizon of the flood, a level in the air below which
everything was stained the dull grey-brown of silt, and
the tree branches were hung with tatters of drift, as
though the flood was still there in ghostly presence.
Above that horizon the spring went on uninterrupted,
the new clear green of the leaves unfolding. It was as
though I sat with my feet in one world and my head in
another. And so with the mud still drying on the floors,
I resumed my connection with the Camp.

Other creatures had worse luck getting started that
spring than I did. On the Monday of the rise I watched
a pair of prothonotary warblers hovering and fluttering
around their nest hole near the top of a box elder snag.
The snag stood on the bank directly below the porch of
the Camp, its top about level with the floor. And so
that night when the river crept into the Camp it had
already filled the warblers' nest. When I came back after the water went down the birds were back. They
nested again in the same hole. And then sometime
around the middle of June the snag blew over. Since
then I believe that no pair has nested near the Camp,
though they nest around the slew across the river and
I often see them feeding here.

That spring a pair of phoebes nested under the eaves
in front of the house just above the door to the screened
porch. A dead elm branch reaching over the porch made
them a handy place to sit and watch for insects. I would
often pause in my writing or reading to watch them fly
out, pick an insect out of the air, and return to the
branch. Sometimes I could hear their beaks snap when
they made a catch.

A pair of starlings was nesting in a woodpecker hole
in a maple down the bank in front of my writing table
and a pair of crested flycatchers in another hollow
maple a few yards upstream. Titmice were in a woodpecker hole in the dead locust near the kitchen door.
High up in an elm, in the fork of a branch hanging over
the driveway, pewees built their neat cup of a nest and

covered the outside with lichens, so that it looked strangely permanent and ancient, like a small rock.

Wood thrushes lived in the thicker woods upriver. They never came near the house while I was there, but their music did, as though their feeling toward me was both timid and generous. One of the unforgettable voices of this place is their exultant fluting rising out of the morning shadows.

On two separate days, while I sat at work, a hummingbird came in through a hole in the rotted porch screen to collect spiderwebs for his nest. He would stand in the air, deliberate as a harvester, and gather the web in his beak with a sort of winding motion.

Later, in July, I would often watch a red-bellied woodpecker who hunted along the tree trunks on this side of the river to feed his young in a hollow snag on the far side. He would work his way slowly up the trunks of the sycamores, turning his head to the side, putting his eye close to the trunk to search under the loose bark scales. And then he would fly to the far side of the river, where his snag jutted up over the top of a big willow. With the binoculars I could see him perch at his hole and feed his nestlings.

For the first time in all my staying at the Camp I had a pair of binoculars, and perhaps more than anything else during that time, they enlarged and intensified my awareness of the place. With their help I began to know the warblers. At a distance these little birds usually look drab, and the species are hardly distinguishable, but the binoculars show them to be beautifully colored and marked, and wonderfully various in their kinds. There is always something deeply enticing and pleasing to me in the sight of them. Perhaps because I was only dimly aware of them for so long, I always see them at first with a certain unexpectedness, and with the sense of gratitude that one feels for any goodness unearned and almost missed. In their secretive worlds of treetop and undergrowth, they seem among the most remote of the wild creatures. They see little of us, and we see even

less of them. I think of them as being aloof somehow
from common life. Certain of the most beautiful of
them, I am sure, have lived and died for generations in
some of our woods without being recognized by a human being.

But the binoculars not only give access to knowledge
of lives that are usually elusive and distant; they make
possible a peculiar imaginative association with those
lives. While opening and clarifying the remote, they
block out the immediate. Where one is is no longer apparent. It is as though one stood at the window of a
darkened room, lifted into a world that cannot be
reached except by flying. The treetops are no longer a
ceiling, but a spacious airy zone full of perching places
and nervously living lights and shadows. One sees not
just the bird, but something of how it is to *be* the bird.
One's imagination begins to reach and explore into the
sense of how it would be to be without barriers, to fly
over the river, to perch at the frailest, most outward
branchings of the trees.

In those days I began the long difficult realization of
the complexity of the life of this place. Until then—at
the level of consciousness, at least—I had thoughtlessly
accepted the common assumption of my countrymen
that the world is merely an inert surface that man lives
on and uses. I don't believe that I had yet read anything
on the subject of ecology. But I had read Thoreau and
Gilbert White and a little of Fabre, and from seeing
natural history displays I knew the concept of the habi-
tat group. And that summer, I remember, I began to
think of myself as living within rather than upon the
life of the place. I began to think of my life as one
among many, and one kind among many kinds. I began
to see how little of the beauty and the richness of the
world is of human origin, and how superficial and crude
and destructive—even self-destructive—is man's con-
ception of himself as the owner of the land and the
master of nature and the center of the universe. The
Camp with its strip of riverbank woods, like all other

places of the earth, stood under its own widening column of infinity, in the neighborhood of the stars, lighted a little, with them, within the element of darkness. It was more unknown than known. It was populated by creatures whose ancestors were here long before my ancestors came, and who had been more faithful to it than I had been, and who would live as well the day after my death as the day before.

Seen as belonging there with other native things, my own nativeness began a renewal of meaning. The sense of belonging began to turn around. I saw that if I belonged here, which I felt I did, it was not because anything here belonged to me. A man might own a whole county and be a stranger in it. If I belonged *in* this place it was because I belonged *to* it. And I began to understand that so long as I did not know the place fully, or even adequately, I belonged to it only partially. That summer I began to see, however dimly, that one of my ambitions, perhaps my governing ambition, was to belong fully to this place, to belong as the thrushes and the herons and the muskrats belonged, to be altogether at home here. That is still my ambition. I have made myself willing to be entirely governed by it. But now I have come to see that it proposes an enormous labor. It is a spiritual ambition, like goodness. The wild creatures belong to the place by nature, but as a man I can belong to it only by understanding and by virtue. It is an ambition I cannot hope to succeed in wholly, but I have come to believe that it is the most worthy of all.

Whenever I could during that summer I would come to the Camp—usually on Sundays, and on days when it was too wet for farm work. I remember vividly the fine feeling I would have, starting out after breakfast with a day at the river ahead of me. The roadsides would be deep in the fresh clear blue of chicory flowers that in the early morning sun appeared to give off a light of their own. And then I would go down into the fog that lay deep in the valley, and begin work. Slowly

the sun would burn through the fog, and brighten the
wet foliage along the riverbanks in a kind of second
dawn. When I got tired of reading or writing I would
cut weeds around the house, or trim the trees to open
up the view of the river. Or I would take a walk into
the woods.

And as before, as always, there was the persistent
consciousness of the river, the sense of sitting at the
edge of a great opening passing through the country
from the Appalachians to the Gulf of Mexico. The
river is the ruling presence of this place. Here one is
always under its influence. The mind, no matter how
it concentrates on other things, is never quite free of it,
is always tempted and tugged at by the nearness of the
water and the clear space over it, ever widening and
deepening into the continent. Its life, in the long warm
days of summer when the water is low, is as leisurely
and self-preoccupied as the life of a street in a country
town. Fish and fishermen pass along it, and so do the
kingfishers and the herons. Rabbits and squirrels and
groundhogs come down in the late afternoon to drink.
The birds crisscross between shores from morning to
night. The muskrats graze the weed patches or browse
the overhanging willows or carry whole stalks of green
corn down out of the fields to the water's edge. Molting
wood ducks skulk along the banks, hiding under the
willows and behind the screens of grapevines. But of
all the creatures, except the fish, I think the swallows
enjoy the river most. Whole flocks of barn swallows and
rough wings will spend hours in the afternoon and
evening circling and dipping over the water, feeding,
bathing, drinking—and rejoicing, too, as I steadfastly
believe, for I cannot imagine that anything could fly as
splendidly as the swallows and not enjoy it.

One afternoon as I was sitting at my worktable on the
porch a towboat came up with two barges loaded with
sand. A man and a boy sat on the edge of the bow of
the head barge, their feet hanging over the water. They
were absorbed in their talk, remote from observance,

the river world wholly surrounding and containing them, like the boatmen in the paintings of George Caleb Bingham. For the moment they belonged to movement and I to stillness; they were bound in kinship with the river, which is always passing, and I in kinship with the trees, which stand still. I watched them out of sight, intensely aware of them and of their unawareness of me. It is an eloquent memory, full of the meaning of this river.

And on those days, as on all the days I have spent here, I was often accompanied by the thought of Curran Mathews. When I am here, I am always near the thought of him, whether I think about him or not. For me, his memory will always be here, as indigenous and congenial as the sycamores. As long as I am here, I think, he will not be entirely gone. Shortly after the May flood of that year of 1961 I was walking in the weeds on the slope above the original site of the Camp, and I came unexpectingly on a patch of flowers that he had planted there thirty years before. They were trillium, lily of the valley, woodland phlox, Jacob's-ladder, and some ferns. Except for the lily of the valley, these flowers are native to the woods of this area— though they apparently had not returned to this stretch of the riverbank since it was cleared and plowed. And so in digging them up and bringing them here, Curran was assisting amiably in the natural order. They have remained through all the years because they belong here; it is their nature to live in such a place as this. But his pleasure in bringing them here is an addition to them that does not hamper them at all. All their lives they go free of him. Because the river had carried the Camp some distance from the old site, leaving the flowers out of the way of our usual comings and goings, I had never seen them before. They appeared at my feet like some good news of Curran, fresh as if he had spoken it to me, tidings of a day when all was well with him.

Another insistent presence that summer was that of time. The Camp was rapidly aging and wearing out. It had suffered too much abandonment, had been forgotten too much, and the river had flowed into it too many times. Its floors were warped and tilted. The roof leaked where a falling elm branch had punched through the tin. Some of the boards of the walls had begun to rot where the wet weeds leaned against them. What was purposive in it had begun to be overtaken by the necessary accidents of time and weather. Decay revealed its kinship with the earth, and it seemed more than ever to belong to the riverbank. The more the illusion of permanence fell away from it, the easier it fit into the flux of things, as though it entered the fellowship of birds' nests and of burrows. But as a house, it was a failed boat. As a place to sit and work, it was a flimsy, slowly tilting shelf. As a shelter, it was like a tree.

And the day was coming when I would leave again. And again I did not know when I would be back. But this time I did consciously intend to come back. Tanya and I had even begun to talk of building a house someday there on the riverbank, although the possibility seemed a long way off, and the plan was more to comfort ourselves with than to act on. But the plan, because it represented so deep a desire, was vivid to us and we believed in it. Near the original site of the Camp were two fine sycamores, and we thought of a house standing on the slope above them, looking down between them at the river. As a sort of farewell gesture, and as a pledge, I cut down some box elders and elms whose branches had begun to grow obstructively into the crowns of the sycamores. And so, before leaving, I made the beginning of a future that I hoped for and dimly foresaw.

On the twelfth of March the following spring, a letter came to us in Florence, Italy, saying that the river was in the Camp again. Far away as I was, the letter made me strangely restless and sad. I could clearly imagine the look of it. The thought of inundation filled me: the river claiming its valley, making it over again and again —the Camp, my land creature, inhabited by water. The thought, at that distance, that what I knew might be changed filled me and held me in abeyance, as the river filled and held the Camp.

After the year in Europe we lived in New York, and I taught at New York University. We had a second child by then, a boy. In the winter of 1963, I accepted a teaching job at the University of Kentucky to begin in the fall of the following year. That suited us. Our hopes and plans had already turned us back toward Kentucky. We had already spent several years living in other places, and after a second year in New York we would be ready to think of settling down at home.

We returned to Kentucky when school was out that year to spend the summer. And encouraged by the prospect that my relation to the place might soon be permanent, I planned to rebuild the Camp. For one reason, I would be needing a place set aside to do my work in. Another reason, and the main one, was that I needed to preserve the Camp as an idea and a possibility here where it had always been. So many of the good days of my life had been lived here that I could not willingly separate myself from it.

At first I considered repairing the Camp as it stood. But as I looked it over it appeared to be too far gone to be worth the effort and money I would have to spend on it. Besides, it was too near the river; as the watershed deteriorated more and more through misuse, the spring rises had begun to come over the floors too often. Much as I still valued it, the old house had become a relic, and there were no more arguments in its favor. And so on the sixth of June, 1963, I began the work of tearing it down and clearing a place farther up the bank to build it back again. That afternoon I took out the partition between the two rooms, and then cut down the elm that stood where the new building was to be.

The next afternoon I cleared the weeds and bushes off the building site, and with that my sadness at parting with the old house began to give way to the idea of the new. I was going to build the new house several feet higher up the slope than the old one, and to place it so that it would look out between the two big sycamores. Unlike a wild place, a human place gone wild can be strangely forbidding and even depressing. But that afternoon's work made me feel at home here again. My plans suddenly took hold of me, and I began to visualize the new house as I needed it to be and as I thought it ought to look. My work had made the place inhabitable, had set my imagination free in it. I began again to belong to it.

During the next several days I worked back and forth between the old and the new, tearing down and preparing to build. The tearing down was slow work, for I wanted to save and reuse as much of the old lumber as I could, and the floods had rusted all the nails tight in their holes. The sediment of the flood of 1937 still lay on the tops of the rafters. And on the sheeting under the tin of the roof I found the wallpaper the boards had worn when they stood in the walls of the old family house up on the top of the hill. I squared the outlines of the new house on the slope—measuring off a single room twelve by sixteen feet, and a porch eight by eight feet—and dug the holes for the posts it would stand on.

By June 18 I was ready to begin building, and that day two carpenters, friends of mine I had hired to help me, came early in the morning, and we began work. By the night of the twenty-fifth the new house was up, the roof and siding were on, and from that day I continued the work by myself. The old Camp provided the roof, the floor, and three walls of the new, as well as the two doors and some windows. This dependence on the old materials determined to a considerable extent the shape of the new house, for we would shorten or lengthen the dimensions as we went along in accordance with the lengths of the old boards. And so the new house was a true descendant of the old, as the old in its time was the descendant of one still older.

That summer I was deep into the writing on a long book called *A Place on Earth*. And as soon as the

heavier work on the house was done and I no longer
needed the carpenters, I returned to work on the book,
writing in the mornings and continuing work on the
house in the afternoons. I nailed battens over the cracks
between the boards, braced the underpinnings, made
screens and screen doors and shutters and steps, painted
the roof and the outside walls. At the end of the summer I had a satisfactory nutshell of a house, green-
roofed and brown-walled, that seemed to fit well enough
into the place. Standing on its long legs, it had a peering,
aerial look, as though built under the influence of trees.
But it was heron-like, too, and made for wading at the
edge of the water.

The most expensive member of the new house was a
big window, six feet by four and a half feet, with forty
panes. This was the eye of the house, and I put it in the
wall facing the river and built a long worktable under
it. In addition, three window sashes from the old Camp
were set into each of the end walls. And so the house
became a container of shifting light, the sunlight entering by the little windows in the east wall in the morning,
and by those in the west wall in the afternoon, and the
steadier light from the northward-staring big window
over the worktable.

When I began tearing down the old Camp a pair of
phoebes was nesting as usual under one of the eaves.
Four eggs were already in the nest. I took an old shutter
and fixed a little shelf and a sort of porch roof on it,
and nailed it to a locust tree nearby, and set the nest
with its eggs carefully on it. As I feared, the old birds
would have nothing to do with it. The nest stayed where
I had put it for another year or so, a symbol of the
ended possibilities of the old Camp, and then it blew
away.

As I wrote through the mornings of the rest of that
summer, a green heron would often be fishing opposite
me on the far bank. An old willow had leaned down
there until it floated on the water, reaching maybe
twenty feet out from the bank. The tree was still living,

nearly the whole length of it covered with leafy sprouts. It was dead only at the outer end, which bent up a few inches above the surface of the river. And it was there that the heron fished. He stooped a little, leaning a little forward, his eyes stalking the river as it flowed down and passed beneath him. His attention would be wonderfully concentrated for minutes at a stretch, he would stand still as a dead branch on the trunk of his willow, and then he would itch and have to scratch among his feathers with his beak. When prey swam within his reach, he would crouch, tilt, pick it deftly out of the water, sit back, swallow. Once I saw him plunge headlong into the water and flounder out with his minnow— as if the awkward flogging body had been literally yanked off its perch by the accurate hunger of the beak. When a boat passed he did not fly, but walked calmly back into the shadows among the sprouts of the willow and stood still.

Another bird I was much aware of that summer was the sycamore warbler. Nearly every day I would see one feeding in the tall sycamores in front of the house, or when I failed to see the bird I would hear its song. This is a bird of the tall trees, and he lives mostly in their highest branches. He loves the sycamores. He moves through their crowns, feeding, and singing his peculiar quaking seven-note song, a voice passing overhead like the sun. I am sure I had spent many days of my life with this bird going about his business high over my head, and I had never been aware of him before. This always amazes me; it has happened to me over and over; for years I will go in ignorance of some creature that will later become important to me, as though we are slowly drifting toward each other in time, and then it will suddenly become as visible to me as a star. It is at once almost a habit. After the first sighting I see it often. I become dependent on it, and am uneasy when I do not see it. In the years since I first saw it here and heard its song, the sycamore warbler has come to hold this sort of power over me. I never hear it approaching through the white branches of its trees that I don't stop and listen; or I get the binoculars and watch him as he makes his way from one sycamore to another along the riverbank, a tiny gray bird with a yellow throat, singing from white branch to white branch, among the leaf lights and shadows. When I hear his song for the first time in the spring, I am deeply touched and reassured. It has come to be the most characteristic voice of this place. He is the Camp's emblem bird, as the sycamore is its emblem tree.

From the old Camp the new Camp inherited the fate of a river house. High up as I had built it, I hadn't been able to move it beyond the reach of the river; there was not room enough here below the road to do that. Like the old house, the new was doomed to make its way in the water—to be a failed boat, and survive by luck. The first spring after it was built the river rose more than two feet over the floor. When the water went down, my uncle hosed out the silt and made the place clean again, and when I came back from New York later in the spring it looked the way it had before. But the idea of it had changed. If it had been built in the hope that the river would never rise into it and in the fear that it would, it now lived in the fact that the river had and in the likelihood that it would again. Like all river houses, it had become a stoical house. Sitting in it, I never forget that I am within the reach of an awesome power. It is a truthful house, not indulging the illusion of the permanence of human things. To be here always is not its hope. Long-legged as it is, it is responsive to the natural vibrations. When the dog scratches under the table there is a tremor in the rafters.

Our return from New York in early June of 1964 changed our lives. We were coming back to Kentucky this time with the intention of staying and making a home. Our plans were still unsettled, but our direction was clear. For the first time, we were beginning to have a foreseeable future. From then on, my relation to my native country here might be interrupted occasionally, but it would not be broken. For the summer, we would stay on the farm and I would spend the days working at the Camp, as before.

The previous summer, when I had moved the phoebes' nest from under the eaves of the old Camp before tearing it down, I had said to myself that it would be a good omen if the birds should nest the next year at the new Camp. And they did, building their mossy nest under the roof of the porch. I felt honored by this, as though my work had been received into the natural order. The phoebes had added to its meaning. Later in the summer a pair of Carolina wrens also nested under the porch roof. Instead of one room, I had begun to have a house of apartments where several different kinds of life went on together. And who is to say that one kind is more possible or natural here than another? My writing and the family life of the phoebes go along here together, in a kind of equality.

In that summer of 1964 one of my first jobs was to insulate the Camp, and to wall and ceil it on the inside with six-inch tongue and groove. Once that was done, I resumed my mornings of writing. The afternoons I often spent working around the Camp, or reading, or walking in the woods. As fall approached I had a bottle-gas heater and a two-burner cooking stove installed, which made the Camp ready for cold weather use and for what is known as batching.

We still were unsure what shape our life in Kentucky was going to take, and so we had rented a furnished house in Lexington for the winter. Since I was still at work on my book, the plan was that I would do my teaching at the university on Tuesdays, Wednesdays, and Thursdays, and then drive down to the Camp to write during the other four days. Difficult as this was, it seemed the best way of assuring the quiet and the concentration that I needed for my work. But as a sort of by-product, it also made for the most intense and prolonged experience of the Camp and the river that I had ever known. In many ways that was to be a most

critical time for me. Before it was over it would make
a deep change in my sense of myself, and in my sense
of the country I was born in.

From the beginning of September, when school started, until the first of May, when it was over, I would
leave Lexington after supper Thursday night and stay
at the Camp through Monday afternoon. Occasionally
I would stay for some meeting or other at the university
on into Thursday night, and those late drives are the
ones I remember best. I would leave the university and
drive across Lexington and the suburbs, and then the
sixty miles through the country and down along the
river to the Camp. As I went, the roads would grow less
traveled, the night quieter and lonelier, the darkness
broken by fewer lights. I would reach the Camp in the
middle of the night, the country quiet and dark all
around when I turned off the car engine and the head-
lights. I would hear an owl calling, or the sound of the
small stream on the far bank tumbling into the river. I
would go in, light the lamp and the stove, read until the
room warmed, and then sleep. The next morning I
would be at work on my book at the table under the
window. It was always a journey from the sound of public voices to the sound of a private quiet voice rising
falteringly out of the roots of my mind, that I listened
carefully in the silence to hear. It was a journey from
the abstract collective life of the university and the city
into the intimate country of my own life. It is only in a
country that is well known, full of familiar names and
places, full of life that is always changing, that the mind
goes free of abstractions, and renews itself in the presence of the creation, that so persistently eludes human
comprehension and human law. It is only in the place
that one belongs to, intimate and familiar, long watched
over, that the details rise up out of the whole and become visible: the hawk stoops into the clearing before
one's eyes; the wood drake, aloof and serene in his
glorious plumage, swims out of his hiding place.

One clear morning as the fall was coming on I saw

a chipmunk sunning on a log, as though filling himself
with light and warmth in preparation for his winter
sleep. He was wholly preoccupied with the sun, for
though I watched him from only a few steps away he
did not move. And while he mused or dozed rusty-
golden sycamore leaves bigger than he was were falling
all around him.

With the approach of winter the country opened.
Around the Camp the limits of seeing drew back like
the eyelids of a great eye. The foliage that since spring
had enclosed it slowly fell away, and the outlook from
its windows came to include the neighboring houses. It
was as though on every frosty night the distances stole
up nearer.

On the last morning of October, waking, I looked out
the window and saw a fisherman in a red jacket fishing
alone in his boat tied against the far bank. He sat deeply
quiet and still, unmoved as a tree by my rising and the
other events that went on around him. There was something heron-like in his intent waiting upon what the day
might bring him out of the dark. In his quietness and
patience he might have been the incarnation of some
river god, at home among all things, awake while I had
slept.

One bright warm day in November it was so quiet
that I could hear the fallen leaves ticking, like a light
rain, as they dried and contracted, scraping their points
and edges against each other. That day I saw the first
sapsuckers, which are here only in the winter.

Another day I woke to see the trees below the house
full of birds: chickadees, titmice, juncos, bluebirds,
jays. They had found a red screech owl asleep in a hollow in one of the water maples. It was a most noisy
event, and it lasted a long time. The bluebirds would
hover, fluttering like sparrow hawks, over the owl's
hole, looking in. The titmice would perch on the very lip
of the hole and scold and then, as if in fear of their own
bravery, suddenly startle away. They all flew away and
came back again two or three times. Everybody seemed

to have a great backlog of invective to hurl down upon the head of the owl, who apparently paid no attention at all—at least when I climbed up and looked in he paid no attention to me.

I believe that the owl soon changed his sleeping place; when I next looked in he was gone. But for days afterward the birds of the neighborhood pretended he was still there, and would stop in passing to enact a sort of ritual of outrage and fright. The titmice seemed especially susceptible to the fascination of that hole. They would lean over it, yell down into it, and then spring away in a spasm of fear. They seemed to be scaring themselves for fun, like children playing around a deserted house. And yet for both birds and children there must be a seriousness in such play; they mimic fear in order to be prepared for it when it is real.

While I was eating breakfast the morning after the birds' discovery of the owl, I heard several times a voice that I knew was strange to this place. I was reading as I ate, and at first I paid little attention. But the voice persisted, and when I put my mind to it I thought it must be that of a goose. I went out with the binoculars, and saw two blue geese, the young of that year, on the water near the far bank. Though the morning was clear and the sun well up, there was a light fog blowing over the river, thickening and thinning out and thickening again, making it difficult to see, but I made out their markings clearly enough. While I watched they waded out on shore at a place where the bank had slipped, preened their feathers, and drank, and after about fifteen minutes flew away.

That afternoon I found them again in the same slip where I had seen them in the morning. I paddled the canoe within twenty feet of them, and then they only flew out onto the water a short distance away. I thought that since these birds nest to the north of Hudson Bay and often fly enormous distances in migration, I might have been the first man these had ever seen. Not wanting to call attention to them and so get them shot, I went on across the river and walked into the bottom on the far side. I spent some time there, looking at the wood ducks and some green-winged teal on the slews, and when I returned to the canoe a little before five the geese were gone. But my encounter with them cast a new charm on my sense of the place. They made me realize that the geography of this patch of riverbank takes in much of the geography of the world. It is under the influence of the Arctic, where the winter birds go in summer, and of the tropics, where the summer birds go in winter. It is under the influence of forests and of croplands and of strip mines in the Appalachians, and it feels the pull of the Gulf of Mexico. How many nights have the migrants loosened from their guide stars and descended here to rest or to stay for a season or to die and enter this earth? The geography of this place is airy and starry as well as earthy and watery. It has been arrived at from a thousand other places, some as far away as the poles. I have come here from great distances myself, and am resigned to the knowledge that I cannot go without leaving it better or worse. Here as well as any place I can look out my window and see the world. There are lights that arrive here from deep in the universe. A man can be provincial only by being blind and deaf to his province.

In December the winter cold began. Early in the mornings when it would be clear and cold the drift logs going down the channel would be white with frost, not having moved except as the current moved all night, as firmly embedded in the current, almost, as in the ground. A sight that has always fascinated me, when the river is up and the water swift, is to see the birds walking about, calmly feeding, on the floating logs and the mats of drift as they pass downward, slowly spinning in the currents. The ducks, too, like to feed among the drift in the channel at these times. I have seen mallards drift down, feeding among the uprooted tree trunks and the cornstalks and the rafted brush, and then fly back upstream to drift down again.

A voice I came to love and listen for on the clear cold mornings was that of the Carolina wren. He would be quick and busy, on the move, singing as he went. Unlike the calls of the other birds, whose songs, if they sang at all, would be faltering and halfhearted in the cold, the wren's song would come big and clear, filling the air of the whole neighborhood with energy, as though he could not bear to live except in the atmosphere of his own music.

Toward the end of that December a gray squirrel began building a nest in a hollow sycamore near the house. He seemed unable or unwilling to climb the trunk of the sycamore; in all the time I watched him he never attempted to do so. He always followed the same complicated route to his nest: up a grapevine, through the top of an elm and then, by a long leap, into the sycamore. On his way down this route offered him no difficulties, but the return trip, when he carried a load of sycamore leaves in his mouth, seemed fairly risky. The big leaves gave him a good deal of trouble; he frequently stopped and worked with his forepaws to make the load more compact. But because he persisted in carrying as big loads as he could, his forward vision seemed usually to be blocked altogether. I believe that his very exacting leaps were made blind, by memory, after a bit of nervous calculation beforehand. When he moved with a load of leaves, apparently because of the obstruction of his vision, he was always extremely wary, stopping often to listen and look around.

I remember one night of snow, so cold that the snow squeaked under my feet when I went out. The valley was full of moonlight; the fields were dazzling white, the woods deep black, the shadows of the trees printed heavily on the snow. And it was quiet everywhere. As long as I stood still there was not a sound.

That winter a pair of flickers drilled into the attic and slept there. Sometimes at night, after I went to bed, I could hear them stirring. But contrary to my sense of economy—though, I suppose, in keeping with theirs—

they did not make do with a single hole, but bored one in one gable and one in the other. I shared my roof with them until the cold weather ended, and then evicted them. Later I put up a nesting box for them, which was promptly taken over by starlings.

One sunny morning of high water in April while I sat at work, keeping an eye on the window as usual, there were nineteen coot, a pair of wood ducks, and two pairs of blue-winged teal feeding together near the opposite bank. They fed facing upstream, working against the current, now and then allowing themselves to be carried downstream a little way, then working upstream again. After a while the four teal climbed out onto a drift log caught in the bushes near the shore. For some time they sat sunning and preening there. And then the log broke loose and began to drift again. The four birds never moved. They rode it down the river and out of sight. They accepted this accident of the river as much as a matter of fact as if it had been a purpose of theirs. Able both to swim and to fly, they made a felicity of traveling by drift log, as if serendipity were merely a way of life with them.

On the tenth of April, I woke at about six o'clock, and the first sound I heard was the song of the sycamore warbler, returned from the South. With that my thoughts entered spring. I went into the woods and found the bloodroot in bloom. Curran's flowers were coming up on the slope beside the house. In the warm evening I noticed other spring music: the calling of doves, and the slamming of newly hung screen doors.

During that winter I had spent many days and nights of watchfulness and silence here. I had learned the power of silence in a place—silence that is the imitation of absence, that permits one to be present as if absent, so that the life of the place goes its way undisturbed. It proposes an ideal of harmlessness. A man should be in the world as though he were not in it, so that it will be no worse because of his life. His obligation may not be to make "a better world," but the world certainly requires of him that he make it no worse. That, at least, was man's moral circumstance before he began his ruinous attempt to "improve" on the creation; now, perhaps, he is under an obligation to leave it better than he found it, by undoing some of the effects of his meddling and restoring its old initiatives—by making his absence the model of his presence.

But there was not only the power of silence; there was the power of attentiveness, of permanence of interest. By coming back to Kentucky and renewing my devotion to the Camp and the river valley, I had, in a sense, made a marriage with the place. I had estabilshed a trust, and within the assurance of the trust the place had begun to reveal its life to me in moments of deep intimacy and beauty. I had to come here unequivocally, accepting the place as my fate and privilege, before I could see it with clarity. I had become worthy to see what I had inherited by being born here. I had been a native; now I was beginning to belong. There is no word—certainly not *native* or *citizen*—to suggest the state I mean, that of belonging willingly and gladly and with some fullness of knowledge to a place. I had ceased to be a native as men usually are, merely by chance and legality, and had begun to be native in the fashion of the birds and animals; I had begun to be born here in mind and spirit as well as in body.

For some months after our return to Kentucky we assumed that we would settle more or less permanently in Lexington, near the university, and perhaps have a place here in the country to come to for the summers. We had thought of building a couple of more rooms onto the Camp for that purpose, and we had thought of buying a piece of woods out of reach of the river and building there. But in November of that first winter the Lane's Landing property, adjoining the camp on the downriver side, came up for sale, and I was able to buy it. We would, we told ourselves, fix it up a little, use it in the summers, and perhaps settle there permanently some day. The previous owners moved out in

February, and I began spending some of my afternoons there, working to get ready for the carpenters who would work there later on. But on the weekends Tanya and the children would often come down from Lexington, and we would walk over the place, and through the rooms of the house, talking and looking and measuring and planning. And soon we began to see possibilities there that we could not resist. Our life began to offer itself to us in a new way, in the terms of that place, and we could not escape it or satisfy it by anything partial or temporary. We made up our minds to live there. By the morning in April when I first heard the sycamore warbler, we had begun a full-scale overhaul of the house, and I had planted two dozen fruit trees. Early in July, with work completed on only three of the rooms, we moved in. After eight years, our lives enlarged in idea and in concern, our marriage enlarged into a family, we had come back to where we had begun. The Camp, always symbolically the center of our life, had fastened us here at last.

It has been several years now since I first consciously undertook to learn about the natural history of this place. My desire to do this grew out of the sense that the human life of the country is only part of its life, and that in spite of the extreme *effects* of modern man's presence on the land, his relation to it is largely superficial. In spite of all his technical prowess, nothing we have built or done has the permanence, or the congeniality with the earth, of the nesting instincts of the birds.

As soon as I felt a necessity to learn about the nonhuman world, I wished to learn about it in a hurry. And then I began to learn perhaps the most important lesson that nature had to teach me: that I could not learn about her in a hurry. The most important learning, that of experience, can be neither summoned nor sought out. The most worthy knowledge cannot be acquired by what is known as study—though that is necessary, and has its use. It comes in its own good time and in its own way to the man who will go where it lives, and wait, and be ready, and watch. Hurry is beside the point, useless, an obstruction. The thing is to be attentively present. To sit and wait is as important as to move. Patience is as valuable as industry. What is to be known is always there. When it reveals itself to you, or when you come upon it, it is by chance. The only condition is your being there and being watchful.

Though it has come slowly and a little at a time, by bits and fragments sometimes weeks apart, I realize after so many years of just being here that my knowledge of the life of this place is rich, my own life part of its richness. And at that I have only made a beginning. Eternal mysteries are here, and temporal ones too. I expect to learn many things before my life is over, and yet to die ignorant. My most inspiring thought is that this place, if I am to live well in it, requires and deserves a lifetime of the most careful attention. And the day that will finally enlighten me, if it ever comes, will come as the successor of many days spent here unenlightened or benighted entirely. "It requires more than a day's devotion," Thoreau says, "to know and to possess the wealth of a day."

At the same time my days here have taught me the futility of living for the future. Men who drudge all their lives in order to retire happily are the victims of a cheap spiritual fashion invented for their enslavement. It is no more possible to live in the future than it is to live in the past. If life is not now, it is never. It is impossible to imagine "how it will be," and to linger over that task is to prepare a disappointment. The tomorrow I hope for may very well be worse than today. There is a great waste and destructiveness in our people's desire to "get somewhere." I myself have traveled several thousand miles to arrive at Lane's Landing, five miles from where I was born, and the knowledge I gained by my travels was mainly that I was born into the same world as everybody else.

Days come to me here when I rest in spirit, and am involuntarily glad. I sense the adequacy of the world, and believe that everything I need is here. I do not strain after ambition or heaven. I feel no dependence on tomorrow. I do not long to travel to Italy or Japan, but only across the river or up the hill into the woods.

And somewhere back of all this, in a relation too intricate and profound to trace out, is the life that Curran Mathews lived here before me. Perhaps he, too, experienced holy days here. Perhaps he only sensed their possibility. But if he had not come here and made a firm allegiance with this place, it is likely that I never would have. I am his follower and his heir. "For an inheritance to be really great," René Char says, "the hand of the deceased must not be seen." The Camp is my inheritance from Curran Mathews, and though certain of his meanings continue in it, his hand is not on it. As an inheritance, he touched it only as a good man touches the earth—to cherish and augment it. Where his hand went to the ground one forgotten day the flowers rise up spring after spring.

Now it is getting on toward the end of March. Just as the grass had started to grow and the jonquils were ready to bloom, we had a foot of snow and more cold. Today it is clear and thawing, but the ground is still white. Though the redbird sings his mating song, it is still winter, and my thoughts keep their winter habits. But soon there will come a day when, without expecting to, I will hear the clear seven-note song of the sycamore warbler passing over the Camp roof. Something will close and open in my mind like a page turning. It will be another spring.

A NATIVE HILL

Pull down thy vanity, it is not man
Made courage, or made order, or made grace,
   Pull down thy vanity, I say pull down.
Learn of the green world what can be thy place. . . .
                              Ezra Pound, *Canto LXXXI*

I

The hill is not a hill in the usual sense. It has no "other side." It is an arm of Kentucky's central upland known as The Bluegrass; one can think of it as a ridge reaching out from that center, progressively cut and divided, made ever narrower by the valleys of the creeks that drain it. The town of Port Royal in Henry County stands on one of the last heights of this upland, the valleys of two creeks, Gullion's Branch and Cane Run, opening on either side of it into the valley of the Kentucky River. My house backs against the hill's foot where it descends from the town to the river. The river, whose waters have carved the hill and so descended from it, lies within a hundred steps of my door.

Within about four miles of Port Royal, on the upland and in the bottoms upriver, all my grandparents and great-grandparents lived and left such memories as their descendants have bothered to keep. Little enough has been remembered. The family's life here goes back to my mother's great-great-grandfather and to my father's great-grandfather, but of those earliest ones there are

171

only a few vague word-of-mouth recollections. The only place antecedent to this place that has any immediacy to any of us is the town of Cashel in County Tipperary, Ireland, which one of my great-grandfathers left as a boy to spend the rest of his life in Port Royal. His name was James Mathews, and he was a shoemaker. So well did he fit his life into this place that he is remembered, even in the family, as having belonged here. The family's only real memories of Cashel are my own, coming from a short visit I made there five years ago.

And so such history as my family has is the history of its life here. All that any of us may know of ourselves is to be known in relation to this place. And since I did most of my growing up here, and have had most of my most meaningful experiences here, the place and the history, for me, have been inseparable, and there is a sense in which my own life is inseparable from the history and the place. It is a complex inheritance, and I have been both enriched and bewildered by it.

☆

I began my life as the old times and the last of the old-time people were dying out. The Depression and World War II delayed the mechanization of the farms here, and one of the first disciplines imposed on me was that of a teamster. Perhaps I first stood in the role of student before my father's father, who, halting a team in front of me, would demand to know which mule had the best head, which the best shoulder or rump, which was the lead mule, were they hitched right. And there came a time when I knew, and took a considerable pride in knowing. Having a boy's usual desire to play at what he sees men working at, I learned to harness and hitch and work a team. I felt distinguished by that, and took the same pride in it that other boys my age took in their knowledge of automobiles. I seem to have been born with an aptitude for a way of life that was doomed, although I did not understand that at the time. Free of any intuition of its doom, I delighted in it, and learned all I could about it.

That knowledge, and the men who gave it to me, influenced me deeply. It entered my imagination, and gave its substance and tone to my mind. It fashioned in me possibilities and limits, desires and frustrations, that I do not expect to live to the end of. And it is strange to think how barely in the nick of time it came to me. If I had been born five years later I would have begun in a different world, and would no doubt have become a different man.

Those five years made a critical difference in my life, and it is a historical difference. One of the results is that in my generation I am something of an anachronism. I am less a child of my time than the people of my age who grew up in the cities, or than the people who grew up here in my own place five years after I did. In my acceptance of twentieth-century realities there has had to be a certain deliberateness, whereas most of my contemporaries had them simply by being born to them.

☆

In my teens, when I was away at school, I could comfort myself by recalling in intricate detail the fields I had worked and played in, and hunted over, and ridden through on horseback—and that were richly associated in my mind with people and with stories. I could recall even the casual locations of certain small rocks. I could recall the look of a hundred different kinds of daylight on all those places, the look of animals grazing over them, the postures and attitudes and movements of the men who worked in them, the quality of the grass and the crops that had grown on them. I had come to be aware of it as one is aware of one's body; it was present to me whether I thought of it or not.

I believe that this has made for a high degree of particularity in my mental processes. When I have thought of the welfare of the earth, the problems of its health and preservation, the care of its life, I have had this place before me, the part representing the whole more vividly and accurately, making clearer and more pressing demands, than any *idea* of the whole. When I have thought of kindness or cruelty, weariness or exuberance, devotion or betrayal, carelessness or care, doggedness or awkwardness or grace, I have had in my mind's eye the men and women of this place, their faces and gestures and movements. It seems to me that because of this I have a more immediate feeling for abstract principles than many of my contemporaries; the values of principles are more vivid to me.

☆

I have pondered a great deal over a conversation I took part in a number of years ago in one of the offices of New York University. I had lived away from Kentucky for several years—in California, in Europe, in New York City. And now I had decided to go back and take a teaching job at the University of Kentucky, giving up the position I then held on the New York University faculty. That day I had been summoned by one of my superiors at the university, whose intention, I had already learned, was to persuade me to stay on in New York "for my own good."

The decision to leave had cost me considerable difficulty and doubt and hard thought—for hadn't I achieved what had become one of the almost traditional goals of American writers? I had reached the greatest city in the nation; I had a good job; I was meeting other writers and talking to them and learning from them; I had reason to hope that I might take a still larger part in the literary life of that place. On the other hand, I knew I had not escaped Kentucky, and had never really wanted to. I was still writing about it, and had recognized that I would probably need to write about it for the rest of my life. Kentucky was my fate—not an altogether pleasant fate, though it had much that was pleasing in it, but one that I could not leave behind simply by going to another place, and that I therefore felt more and more obligated to meet directly and to understand. Perhaps even more important, I still had a deep love for the place I had been born in, and liked the idea of going back to be part of it again. And that, too, I felt obligated to try to understand. Why should I love one place so much more than any other? What could be the meaning or use of such love?

The elder of the faculty began the conversation by alluding to Thomas Wolfe, who once taught at the same institution. "Young man," he said, "don't you know you can't go home again?" And he went on to speak of the advantages, for a young writer, of living in New York among the writers and the editors and the publishers.

The conversation that followed was a persistence of politeness in the face of impossibility. I knew as well as Wolfe that there is a certain *metaphorical* sense in which you can't go home again—that is, the past is lost to the extent that it cannot be lived in again. I knew perfectly well that I could not return home and be a child, or recover the secure pleasures of childhood. But I knew also that as the sentence was spoken to me it bore a self-dramatizing sentimentality that was absurd. Home —the place, the countryside—was still there, still pretty much as I left it, and there was no reason I could not go back to it if I wanted to.

As for the literary world, I had ventured some distance into that, and liked it well enough. I knew that because I was a writer the literary world would always have an importance for me and would always attract my interest. But I never doubted that the world was more important to me than the literary world; and the world would always be most fully and clearly present to me in the place I was fated by birth to know better than any other.

And so I had already chosen according to the most intimate and necessary inclinations of my own life. But what keeps me thinking of that conversation is the feeling that it was a confrontation of two radically different minds, and that it was a confrontation with significant historical overtones.

I do not pretend to know all about the other man's mind, but it was clear that he wished to speak to me as a representative of the literary world—the world he assumed that I aspired to above all others. His argument was based on the belief that once one had attained the metropolis, the literary capital, the worth of one's origins was canceled out; there simply could be nothing *worth* going back to. What lay behind one had ceased to be a part of life, and had become "subject matter." And there was the belief, long honored among American intellectuals and artists and writers, that a place such as I came from could be returned to only at the price of intellectual death; cut off from the cultural springs of the metropolis, the American countryside is Circe and Mammon. Finally, there was the assumption that the life of the metropolis is *the* experience, the *modern* experience, and that the life of the rural towns, the farms, the wilderness places is not only irrelevant to our time, but archaic as well because unknown or unconsidered by the people who really matter—that is, the urban intellectuals.

I was to realize during the next few years how false and destructive and silly those ideas are. But even then I was aware that life outside the literary world was not without honorable precedent: if there was Wolfe, there was also Faulkner; if there was James, there was also Thoreau. But what I had in my mind that made the greatest difference was the knowledge of the few square miles in Kentucky that were mine by inheritance and by birth and by the intimacy the mind makes with the place it awakens in.

☆

I can ask now why it should be so automatically supposed that a man is wrong when he turns to face what he cannot escape, and permits himself to accept what he has desired. And I know that the answer is that in so turning back I turned directly against the current of intellectual fashion, which for so long in America has paralleled the movement of the population from country to city. At times I have found the going difficult. Though at the time of my return I felt that I was acting in faithfulness to my nature and possibilities, and now am certain that I was, there were many months when virtually none of my friends agreed with me. During the first year I was back in Kentucky, though my work apparently gave no evidence of decline, I received letters warning me against the Village Virus and the attitudes of Main Street, counseling me to remain broad-minded and intellectually aware, admonishing that I should be on the lookout for signs of decay in my work and in my mind. It was feared that I would grow paunchy and join the Farm Bureau.

It is of interest to me that, at the start, I was not at all immune to this sort of thing. I felt an obligation to listen, and to take these warnings to heart. I kept an eye on myself, as though the promised signs of decay might appear at any moment. Even at the first I never really thought they would, but I continued, as though honorbound, to expect them even after I had become sure that they wouldn't. Which is to say that, although I had maintained a vital connection with my origins, I had been enough influenced by the cultural fashion to have become compulsively suspicious both of my origins and of myself for being unwilling to divide myself from them.

I have come finally to see a very regrettable irony in what happened. At a time when originality is more emphasized in the arts, maybe, than ever before, I undertook something truly original—I returned to my origins—and it was generally thought by my literary friends that I had worked my ruin. As far as I can tell, this was simply because *my* originality, my faith in my own origins, had not been anticipated or allowed for by the *fashion* of originality.

☆

What finally freed me from these doubts and suspicions was the insistence in what was happening to me that, far from being bored and diminished and obscured to myself by my life here, I had grown more alive and more conscious than I had ever been.

I had made a significant change in my relation to the place: before, it had been mine by coincidence or accident; now it was mine by choice. My return, which at first had been hesitant and tentative, grew wholehearted and sure. I had come back to stay. I hoped to live here the rest of my life. And once that was settled I began to *see* the place with a new clarity and a new understanding and a new seriousness. Before coming back I had been willing to allow the possibility—which one of my friends insisted on—that I already knew this place as well as I ever would. But now I began to see the real abundance and richness of it. It is, I saw, inexhaustible in its history, in the details of its life, in its possibilities. I walked over it, looking, listening, smelling, touching, alive to it as never before. I listened to the talk of my kinsmen and neighbors as I never had done, alert to their knowledge of the place, and to the qualities and energies of their speech. I began more seriously than ever to learn the names of things—the wild plants and animals, the natural processes, the local places—and to articulate my observations and memories. My language increased and strengthened, and sent my mind into the place like a live root system. And so what has become the usual order of things reversed itself with me; my mind became the root of my life rather than its sublimation. I came to see myself as growing out of the earth like the other native animals and plants. I saw my body and my daily motions as brief coherences and articulations of the energy of the place, which would fall back into the earth like leaves in the autumn.

☆

In this awakening there has been a good deal of pain. When I lived in other places I looked on their evils with the curious eye of a traveler; I was not responsible for them; it cost me nothing to be a critic, for I had not been there long, and I did not feel that I would stay. But here, now that I am both native and citizen, there is no immunity to what is wrong. It is impossible to escape the sense that I am involved in history. What I am has been to a considerable extent determined by what my forefathers were, by how they chose to treat this place while they lived in it; the lives of most of them diminished it, and limited its possibilities, and narrowed its future. And every day I am confronted by the question of what inheritance I will leave. What do I have that I am using up? For it has been our history that each generation in this place has been less welcome to it than the last. There has been less here for them. At each arrival there has been less fertility in the soil, and a larger inheritance of destructive precedent and shameful history.

I am forever being crept up on and newly startled by the realization that my people established themselves here by killing or driving out the original possessors, by the awareness that people were once bought and sold here by my people, by the sense of the violence they have done to their own kind and to each other and to the earth, by the evidence of their persistent failure to serve either the place or their own community in it. I am forced, against all my hopes and inclinations, to regard the history of my people here as the progress of the doom of what I value most in the world: the life and health of the earth, the peacefulness of human communities and households.

And so here, in the place I love more than any other and where I have chosen among all other places to live my life, I am more painfully divided within myself than I could be in any other place.

☆

I know of no better key to what is adverse in our
heritage in this place than the account of "The Battle of
the Fire-Brands," quoted in Collins' *History of Kentucky* "from the autobiography of Rev. Jacob Young, a
Methodist minister." The "Newcastle" referred to is the
present-day New Castle, the county seat of Henry
County. I give the quote in full:

> The costume of the Kentuckians was a hunting
> shirt, buckskin pantaloons, a leathern belt around
> their middle, a scabbard, and a big knife fastened to
> their belt; some of them wore hats and some caps.
> Their feet were covered with moccasins, made of
> dressed deer skins. They did not think themselves
> dressed without their powder-horn and shot-pouch,
> or the gun and the tomahawk. They were ready,
> then, for all alarms. They knew but little. They could
> clear ground, raise corn, and kill turkeys, deer, bears,
> and buffalo; and, when it became necessary, they
> understood the art of fighting the Indians as well as
> any men in the United States.
> Shortly after we had taken up our residence, I was
> called upon to assist in opening a road from the place
> where Newcastle now stands, to the mouth of Ken-
> tucky river. That country, then, was an unbroken
> forest; there was nothing but an Indian trail passing
> the wilderness. I met the company early in the morn-
> ing, with my axe, three days' provisions, and my
> knapsack. Here I found a captain, with about 100
> men, all prepared to labor; about as jovial a company
> as I ever saw, all good-natured and civil. This was
> about the last of November, 1797. The day was cold
> and clear. The country through which the company
> passed was delightful; it was not a flat country, but,
> what the Kentuckians called, rolling ground—was
> quite well stored with lofty timber, and the under-
> growth was very pretty. The beautiful canebrakes
> gave it a peculiar charm. What rendered it most
> interesting was the great abundance of wild turkeys,

deer, bears, and other wild animals. The company worked hard all day, in quiet, and every man obeyed the captain's orders punctually.

About sundown, the captain, after a short address, told us the night was going to be very cold, and we must make very large fires. We felled the hickory trees in great abundance; made great log-heaps, mixing the dry wood with the green hickory; and, laying down a kind of sleepers under the pile, elevated the heap and caused it to burn rapidly. Every man had a water vessel in his knapsack; we searched for and found a stream of water. By this time, the fires were showing to great advantage; so we warmed our cold victuals, ate our suppers, and spent the evening in hearing the hunter's stories relative to the bloody scenes of the Indian war. We then heard some pretty fine singing, considering the circumstances.

Thus far, well; but a change began to take place. They became very rude, and raised the war-whoop. Their shrill shrieks made me tremble. They chose two captains, divided the men into two companies, and commenced fighting with the fire-brands—the log heaps having burned down. The only law for their government was, that no man should throw a brand without fire on it—so that they might know how to dodge. They fought, for two or three hours, in perfect good nature; till brands became scarce, and they began to violate the law. Some were severely wounded, blood began to flow freely, and they were in a fair way of commencing a fight in earnest. At this moment, the loud voice of the captain rang out above the din, ordering every man to retire to rest. They dropped their weapons of warfare, rekindled the fires, and laid down to sleep. We finished our road according to directions, and returned home in health and peace.

☆

The significance of this bit of history is in its utter violence. The work of clearing the road was itself violent. And from the orderly violence of that labor, these men turned for amusement to disorderly violence. They

were men whose element was violence; the only alternatives they were aware of were those within the comprehension of main strength. And let us acknowledge that
these were the truly influential men in the history of
Kentucky, as well as in the history of most of the rest
of America. In comparison to the fatherhood of such as
these, the so-called "founding fathers" who established
our political ideals are but distant cousins. It is not John
Adams or Thomas Jefferson whom we see night after
night in the magic mirror of the television set; we see
these builders of the road from New Castle to the mouth
of the Kentucky River. Their reckless violence has glam-
orized all our trivialities and evils. Their aggressions
have simplified our complexities and problems. They
have cut all our Gordian knots. They have appeared in
all our disguises and costumes. They have worn all our
uniforms. Their war whoop has sanctified our inhu-
manity and ratified our blunders of policy.

To testify to the persistence of their influence, it is
only necessary for me to confess that I read the Reverend Young's account of them with delight; I yield a
considerable admiration to the exuberance and extravagance of their fight with the firebrands; I take a certain
pride in belonging to the same history and the same
place that they belong to—though I know that they
represent the worst that is in us, and in me, and that
their presence in our history has been ruinous, and that
their survival among us promises ruin.

"They knew but little," the observant Reverend says
of them, and this is the most suggestive thing he says. It
is surely understandable and pardonable, under the circumstances, that these men were ignorant by the standards of formal schooling. But one immediately reflects
that the American Indian, who was ignorant by the same
standards, nevertheless knew how to live in the country
without making violence the invariable mode of his relation to it; in fact, from the ecologist's or the conserva-
tionist's point of view, he did it *no* violence. This is because he had, in place of what we would call education,

a fully integrated culture, the content of which was a highly complex sense of his dependence on the earth. The same, I believe, was generally true of the peasants of certain old agricultural societies, particularly in the Orient. They belonged by an intricate awareness to the earth they lived on and by, which meant that they respected it, which meant that they practiced strict economies in the use of it.

The abilities of those Kentucky road builders of 1797 were far more primitive and rudimentary than those of the Stone Age people they had driven out. They could clear the ground, grow corn, kill game, and make war. In the minds and hands of men who "know but little"—or little else—all of these abilities are certain to be destructive, even of those values and benefits their use may be intended to serve.

On such a night as the Reverend Young describes, an Indian would have made do with a small shelter and a small fire. But these road builders, veterans of the Indian War, "felled the hickory trees in great abundance; made great log-heaps . . . and caused [them] to burn rapidly." Far from making a small shelter that could be adequately heated by a small fire, their way was to make no shelter at all, and heat instead a sizable area of the landscape. The idea was that when faced with abundance one should consume abundantly—an idea that has survived to become the basis of our present economy. It is neither natural nor civilized, and even from a "practical" point of view it is to the last degree brutalizing and stupid.

I think that the comparison of these road builders with the Indians, on the one hand, and with Old World peasants on the other, is a most suggestive one. The Indians and the peasants were people who belonged deeply and intricately to their places. Their ways of life had evolved slowly in accordance with their knowledge of their land, of its needs, of their own relation of dependence and responsibility to it. The road builders, on the contrary, were *placeless* people. That is why they "knew but little." Having left Europe far behind, they had not yet in any meaningful sense arrived in America, not yet having *devoted* themselves to any part of it in a way that would produce the intricate knowledge of it necessary to live in it without destroying it. Because they belonged to no place, it was almost inevitable that they should behave violently toward the places they came to. We *still* have not, in any meaningful way, arrived in America. And in spite of our great reservoir of facts and methods, in comparison to the deep earthly wisdom of established peoples we still know but little.

But my understanding of this curiously parabolic fragment of history will not be complete until I have considered more directly that the occasion of this particular violence was the building of a road. It is obvious that one who values the idea of community cannot speak against roads without risking all sorts of absurdity. It must be noticed, nevertheless, that the predecessor to this first road was "nothing but an Indian trail passing the wilderness"—a path. The Indians, then, who had the wisdom and the grace to live in this country for perhaps ten thousands years without destroying or damaging any of it, needed for their travels no more than a footpath; but their successors, who in a century and a half plundered the area of at least half its topsoil and virtually all of its forest, felt immediately that they had to have a road. My interest is not in the question of whether or not they *needed* the road, but in the fact that the road was then, and is now, the most characteristic form of their relation to the country.

The difference between a path and a road is not only the obvious one. A path is little more than a habit that comes with knowledge of a place. It is a sort of ritual of familiarity. As a form, it is a form of contact with a known landscape. It is not destructive. It is the perfect adaptation, through experience and familiarity, of movement to place; it obeys the natural contours; such obstacles as it meets it goes around. A road, on the other hand, even the most primitive road, embodies a resis-

tance against the landscape. Its reason is not simply the
necessity for movement, but haste. Its wish is to *avoid*
contact with the landscape; it seeks so far as possible to
go over the country, rather than through it; its aspiration, as we see clearly in the example of our modern
freeways, is to be a bridge; its tendency is to translate
place into space in order to traverse it with the least
effort. It is destructive, seeking to remove or destroy all
obstacles in its way. The primitive road advanced by the
destruction of the forest; modern roads advance by the
destruction of topography.

That first road from the site of New Castle to the
mouth of the Kentucky River—lost now either by
obsolescence or metamorphosis—is now being crossed
and to some extent replaced by its modern descendant
known as I-71, and I have no wish to disturb the question of whether or not *this* road was needed. I only want
to observe that it bears no relation whatever to the
country it passes through. It is a pure abstraction, built
to serve the two abstractions that are the poles of our
national life: commerce and expensive pleasure. It was
built, not according to the lay of the land, but according
to a blueprint. Such homes and farmlands and wood-
lands as happened to be in its way are now buried under
it. A part of a hill near here that would have caused it
to turn aside was simply cut down and disposed of as
thoughtlessly as the pioneer road builders would have
disposed of a tree. Its form is the form of speed, dissatisfaction, and anxiety. It represents the ultimate in
engineering sophistication, but the crudest possible valu-
ation of life in this world. It is as adequate a symbol of
our relation to our country now as that first road was of
our relation to it in 1797.

☆

But the sense of the past also gives a deep richness
and resonance to nearly everything I see here. It is
partly the sense that what I now see other men that I

have known once saw, and partly that this knowledge
provides an imaginative access to what I do not know. I
think of the country as a kind of palimpsest scrawled
over with the comings and goings of people, the erasure
of time already in process even as the marks of passage
are put down. There are the ritual marks of neighborhood—roads, paths between houses. There are the domestic paths from house to barns and outbuildings and
gardens, farm roads threading the pasture gates. There
are the wanderings of hunters and searchers after lost
stock, and the speculative or meditative or inquisitive
"walking around" of farmers on wet days and Sundays.
There is the spiraling geometry of the rounds of imple-
ments in fields, and the passing and returning scratches
of plows across croplands. Often these have filled an
interval, an opening, between the retreat of the forest
from the virgin ground and the forest's return to ground
that has been worn out and given up. In the woods here
one often finds cairns of stones picked up out of furrows,
gullies left by bad farming, forgotten roads, stone chimneys of houses long rotted away or burned.

☆

Occasionally one stumbles into a coincidence that,
like an unexpected alignment of windows, momentarily
cancels out the sense of historical whereabouts, giving
with an overwhelming immediacy an awareness of the
reality of the past.

The possibility of this awareness is always immanent
in old homesites. It may suddenly bear in upon one at
the sight of old orchard trees standing in the dooryard
of a house now filled with baled hay. It came to me
when I looked out the attic window of a disintegrating
log house and saw a far view of the cleared ridges with
wooded hollows in between, and nothing in sight to reveal the date. Who was I, leaning to the window? When?

It broke upon me one afternoon when, walking in the
woods on one of my family places, I came upon a gap in

a fence, wired shut, but with deep-cut wagon tracks still passing through it under the weed growth and the fallen leaves. Where that thicket stands there was crop ground, maybe as late as my own time. I knew some of the men who tended it; their names and faces were instantly alive in my mind. I knew how it had been with them—how they would harness their mule teams in the early mornings in my grandfather's big barn and come to the woods-rimmed tobacco patches, the mules' feet wet with the dew. And in the solitude and silence that came upon them they would set to work, their water jugs left in the shade of bushes in the fencerows.

As a child I learned the early mornings in these places for myself, riding out in the wagons with the tobacco-cutting crews to those steep fields in the dew-wet shadow of the woods. As the day went on the shadow would draw back under the feet of the trees, and it would get hot. Little whirlwinds would cross the opening, picking up the dust and the dry "ground leaves" of the tobacco. We made a game of running with my grandfather to stand, shoulders scrunched and eyes squinched, in their middles.

Having such memories, I can acknowledge only with reluctance and sorrow that those slopes should never have been broken. Rich as they were, they were too steep. The humus stood dark and heavy over them once; the plow was its doom.

☆

Early one February morning in thick fog and spattering rain I stood on the riverbank and listened to a towboat working its way downstream. Its engines were idling, nudging cautiously through the fog into the Cane Run bend. The end of the head barge emerged finally like a shadow, and then the second barge appeared, and then the towboat itself. They made the bend, increased power, and went thumping off out of sight into the fog again.

Because the valley was so enclosed in fog, the boat with its tow appearing and disappearing again into the muffling whiteness within two hundred yards, the moment had a curious ambiguity. It was as though I was not necessarily myself at all. I could have been my grandfather, in his time, standing there watching, as I knew he had.

II

I start down from one of the heights of the upland, the town of Port Royal at my back. It is a winter day, overcast and still, and the town is closed in itself, humming and muttering a little, like a winter beehive.

The dog runs ahead, prancing and looking back, knowing the way we are about to go. This is a walk well established with us—a route in our minds as well as on the ground. There is a sort of mystery in the establishment of these ways. Any time one crosses a given stretch of country with some frequency, no matter how wanderingly one begins, the tendency is always toward habit. By the third or fourth trip, without realizing it, one is following a fixed path, going the way one went before. After that, one may still wander, but only by deliberation, and when there is reason to hurry, or when the mind wanders rather than the feet, one returns to the old route. Familiarity has begun. One has made a relationship with the landscape, and the form and the symbol and the enactment of the relationship is the path. These paths of mine are seldom worn on the ground. They are habits of mind, directions and turns. They are as personal as old shoes. My feet are comfortable in them.

From the height I can see far out over the country, the long open ridges of the farmland, the wooded notches of the streams, the valley of the river opening beyond, and then more ridges and hollows of the same kind.

Underlying this country, nine hundred feet below the highest ridgetops, more than four hundred feet below the surface of the river, is sea level. We seldom think of it here; we are a long way from the coast, and the sea is alien to us. And yet the attraction of sea level dwells in this country as an ideal dwells in a man's mind. All our rains go in search of it and, departing, they have carved the land in a shape that is fluent and falling. The streams branch like vines, and between the branches the land rises steeply and then rounds and gentles into the long narrowing fingers of ridgeland. Near the heads of the streams even the steepest land was not too long ago farmed and kept cleared. But now it has been given up and the woods is returning. The wild is flowing back like a tide. The arable ridgetops reach out above the gathered trees like headlands into the sea, bearing their human burdens of fences and houses and barns, crops and roads.

Looking out over the country, one gets a sense of the whole of it: the ridges and hollows, the clustered buildings of the farms, the open fields, the woods, the stock ponds set like coins into the slopes. But this is a surface sense, an exterior sense, such as you get from looking down on the roof of a house. The height is a threshold from which to step down into the wooded folds of the land, the interior, under the trees and along the branching streams.

I pass through a pasture gate on a deep-worn path that grows shallow a little way beyond, and then disappears altogether into the grass. The gate has gathered thousands of passings to and fro that have divided like the slats of a fan on either side of it. It is like a fist holding together the strands of a net.

Beyond the gate the land leans always more steeply toward the branch. I follow it down, and then bear left along the crease at the bottom of the slope. I have entered the down-flow of the land. The way I am going is the way the water goes. There is something comfortable and fit-feeling in this, something free in this yielding to gravity and taking the shortest way down.

The mind moves through the watershed as the water moves.

As the hollow deepens into the hill, before it has yet entered the woods, the grassy crease becomes a raw gully, and along the steepening slopes on either side I can see the old scars of erosion, places where the earth is gone clear to the rock. My people's errors have become the features of my country.

It occurs to me that it is no longer possible to imagine how this country looked in the beginning, before the white people drove their plows into it. It is not possible to know what was the shape of the land here in this hollow when it was first cleared. Too much of it is gone, loosened by the plows and washed away by the rain. I am walking the route of the departure of the virgin soil of the hill. I am not looking at the same land the first-comers saw. The original surface of the hill is as extinct as the passenger pigeon. The pristine America that the first white man saw is a lost continent, sunk like Atlantis in the sea. The thought of what was here once and is gone forever will not leave me as long as I live. It is as though I walk knee-deep in its absence.

The slopes along the hollow steepen still more, and I go in under the trees. I pass beneath the surface. I am enclosed, and my sense, my interior sense, of the country becomes intricate. There is no longer the possibility of seeing very far. The distances are closed off by the trees and the steepening walls of the hollow. One cannot grow familiar here by sitting and looking as one can up in the open on the ridge. Here the eyes become dependent on the feet. To see the woods from the inside one must look and move and look again. It is inexhaustible in its standpoints. A lifetime will not be enough to experience it all. Not far from the beginning of the woods, and set deep in the earth in the bottom of the hollow, is a rock-walled pool not a lot bigger than a bathtub. The wall is still nearly as straight and tight as when it was built. It makes a neatly turned narrow horseshoe, the open end downstream. This is a historical ruin, dug here either to catch and hold the water of the little branch, or to collect the water of a spring whose vein broke to the surface here—it is probably no longer possible to know which. The pool is filled with earth now, and grass grows in it. And the branch bends around it, cut down to the bare rock, a torrent after heavy rain, other times bone dry. All that is certain is that when the pool was dug and walled there was deep topsoil on the hill to gather and hold the water. And this high up, at least, the bottom of the hollow, instead of the present raw notch of the stream bed wore the same mantle of soil as the slopes, and the stream was a steady seep or trickle, running most or all of the year. This tiny pool no doubt once furnished water for a considerable number of stock through the hot summers. And now it is only a lost souvenir, archaic and useless, except for the bitter intelligence there is in it. It is one of the monuments to what is lost.

Wherever one goes along the streams of this part of the country, one is apt to come upon this old stonework. There are walled springs and pools. There are the walls built in the steeper hollows where the fences cross or used to cross; the streams have drifted dirt in behind them, so that now where they are still intact they make waterfalls that have scooped out small pools at their feet. And there used to be miles of stone fences, now mostly scattered and sifted back into the ground.

Considering these, one senses a historical patience, now also extinct in the country. These walls were built by men working long days for little wages, or by slaves. It was work that could not be hurried at, a meticulous finding and fitting together, as though reconstructing a previous wall that had been broken up and scattered like puzzle pieces along the stream beds. The wall would advance only a few yards a day. The pace of it could not be borne by most modern men, even if the wages could be afforded. Those men had to move in closer accord with their own rhythms, and nature's, than we do. They had no machines. Their capacities were only those of flesh and blood. They talked as they worked. They joked and laughed. They sang. The work was exacting and heavy and hard and slow. No opportunity for pleasure was missed or slighted. The days and the years were long. The work was long. At the end of this job the next would begin. Therefore, be patient. Such pleasure as there is, is here, now. Take pleasure as it comes. Take work as it comes. The end may never come, or when it does it may be the wrong end.

Now the men who built the walls and the men who had them built have long gone underground to be, along with the buried ledges and the roots and the burrowing animals, a part of the nature of the place in the minds of the ones who come after them. I think of them lying still in their graves, as level as the sills and thresholds of their lives, as though resisting to the last the slant of the ground. And their old walls, too, re-enter nature, collecting lichens and mosses with a patience their builders never conceived of.

Like the pasture gates, the streams are great collectors of comings and goings. The streams go down, and paths always go down beside the streams. For a while I walk along an old wagon road that is buried in leaves—a fragment, beginningless and endless as the middle of a sentence on some scrap of papyrus. There is a cedar whose branches reach over this road, and under the branches I find the leavings of two kills of some bird of prey. The most recent is a pile of blue jay feathers. The other has been rained on and is not identifiable. How little we know. How little of this was intended or expected by any man. The road that has become the grave of men's passages has led to the life of the woods.

> And I say to myself: Here is your road
> without beginning or end, appearing
> out of the earth and ending in it, bearing
> no load but the hawk's kill, and the leaves
> building earth on it, something more
> to be borne. Tracks fill with earth

and return to absence. The road was worn
by men bearing earth along it. They have come
to endlessness. In their passing
they could not stay in, trees have risen
and stand still. It is leading to the dark,
to mornings where you are not. Here
is your road, beginningless and endless as God.

Now I have come down within the sound of the water.
The winter has been rainy, and the hill is full of dark
seeps and trickles, gathering finally, along these creases,
into flowing streams. The sound of them is one of the
elements, and defines a zone. When their voices return
to the hill after their absence during summer and autumn, it is a better place to be. A thirst in the mind is
quenched.

I have already passed the place where water began
to flow in the little stream bed I am following. It broke
into the light from beneath a rock ledge, a thin glittering
stream. It lies beside me as I walk, overtaking me and
going by, yet not moving, a thread of light and sound.
And now from below comes the steady tumble and rush
of the water of Camp Branch—whose nameless camp
was it named for?—and gradually as I descend the
sound of the smaller stream is lost in the sound of the
larger.

The two hollows join, the line of the meeting of the
two spaces obscured even in winter by the trees. But
the two streams meet precisely as two roads. That is, the
stream *beds* do; the one ends in the other. As for the
meeting of the waters, there is no looking at that. The
one flow does not end in the other, but continues in it,
one with it, two clarities merged without a shadow.

All waters are one. This is a reach of the sea, flung
like a net over the hill, and now drawn back to the sea.
And as the sea is never raised in the earthly nets of
fishermen, so the hill is never caught and pulled down
by the watery net of the sea. But always a little of it is.
Each of the gathering strands of the net carries back

some of the hill melted in it. Sometimes, as now, it carries so little that the water seems to flow clear; sometimes it carries a lot and is brown and heavy with it. Whenever greedy or thoughtless men have lived on it, the hill has literally flowed out of their tracks into the bottom of the sea.

There appears to be a law that when creatures have reached the level of consciousness, as men have, they must become conscious of the creation; they must learn how they fit into it and what its needs are and what it requires of them, or else pay a terrible penalty: the spirit of the creation will go out of them, and they will become destructive; the very earth will depart from them and go where they cannot follow.

My mind is never empty or idle at the joinings of streams. Here is the work of the world going on. The creation is felt, alive and intent on its materials, in such places. In the angle of the meeting of the two streams stands the steep wooded point of the ridge, like the prow of an upturned boat—finished, as it was a thousand years ago, as it will be in a thousand years. Its becoming is only incidental to its being. It will be because it is. It has no aim or end except to be. By being, it is growing and wearing into what it will be. The fork of the stream lies at the foot of the slope like hammer and chisel laid down at the foot of a finished sculpture. But the stream is no dead tool; it is alive, it is still at its work. Put your hand to it to learn the health of this part of the world. It is the wrist of the hill.

Perhaps it is to prepare to hear some day the music of the spheres that I am always turning my ears to the music of streams. There is indeed a music in streams, but it is not for the hurried. It has to be loitered by and imagined. Or imagined *toward*, for it is hardly for men at all. Nature has a patient ear. To her the slowest funeral march sounds like a jig. She is satisfied to have the notes drawn out to the length of days or weeks or months. Small variations are acceptable to her, modulations as leisurely as the opening of a flower.

The stream is full of stops and gates. Here it has piled up rocks in its path, and pours over them into a tiny pool it has scooped at the foot of its fall. Here it has been dammed by a mat of leaves caught behind a fallen limb. Here it must force a narrow passage, here a wider one. Tomorrow the flow may increase or slacken, and the tone will shift. In an hour or a week that rock may give way, and the composition will advance by another note. Some idea of it may be got by walking slowly along and noting the changes as one passes from one little fall or rapid to another. But this is a highly simplified and diluted version of the real thing, which is too complex and widespread ever to be actually heard by us. The ear must imagine an impossible patience in order to grasp even the unimaginableness of such music.

But the creation is musical, and this is a part of its music, as bird song is, or the words of poets. The music of the streams is the music of the shaping of the earth, by which the rocks are pushed and shifted downward toward the level of the sea.

And now I find lying in the path an empty beer can. This is the track of the ubiquitous man Friday of all our woods. In my walks I never fail to discover some sign that he has preceded me. I find his empty shotgun shells, his empty cans and bottles, his sandwich wrappings. In wooded places along roadsides one is apt to find, as well, his overtraveled bedsprings, his outcast refrigerator, and heaps of the imperishable refuse of his modern kitchen. A year ago, almost in this same place where I have found his beer can, I found a possum that he had shot dead and left lying, in celebration of his manhood. He is the true American pioneer, perfectly at rest in his assumption that he is the first and the last whose inheritance and fate this place will ever be. Going forth, as he may think, to sow, he only broadcasts his effects.

As I go on down the path alongside Camp Branch, I walk by the edge of croplands abandoned only within my own lifetime. On my left are the south slopes where the woods is old, long undisturbed. On my right, the more fertile north slopes are covered with patches of briars and sumacs and a lot of young walnut trees. Tobacco of an extraordinary quality was once grown here, and then the soil wore thin, and these places were given up for the more accessible ridges that were not so steep, where row cropping made better sense anyway. But now, under the thicket growth, a mat of bluegrass has grown to testify to the good nature of this ground. It was fine dirt that lay here once, and I am far from being able to say that I could have resisted the temptation to plow it. My understanding of what is best for it is the tragic understanding of hindsight, the awareness that I have been taught what was here to be lost by the loss of it.

We have lived by the assumption that what was good for us would be good for the world. And this has been based on the even flimsier assumption that we could know with any certainty what was good even for us. We have fulfilled the danger of this by making our personal pride and greed the standard of our behavior toward the world—to the incalculable disadvantage of the world and every living thing in it. And now, perhaps very close to too late, our great error has become clear. It is not only our own creativity—our own capacity for life— that is stifled by our arrogant assumption; the creation itself is stifled.

We have been wrong. We must change our lives, so that it will be possible to live by the contrary assumption that what is good for the world will be good for us. And that requires that we make the effort to *know* the world and to learn what is good for it. We must learn to co-operate in its processes, and to yield to its limits. But even more important, we must learn to acknowledge that the creation is full of mystery; we will never entirely understand it. We must abandon arrogance and stand in awe. We must recover the sense of the majesty of creation, and the ability to be worshipful in its presence. For I do not doubt that it is only on the condition of humility and reverence before the world that our species will be able to remain in it.

Standing in the presence of these worn and abandoned fields, where the creation has begun its healing without the hindrance or the help of man, with the voice of the stream in the air and the woods standing in silence on all the slopes around me, I am deep in the interior not only of my place in the world, but of my own life, its sources and searches and concerns. I first came into these places following the men to work when I was a child. I knew the men who took their lives from such fields as these, and their lives to a considerable extent made my life what it is. In what came to me from them there was both wealth and poverty, and I have been a long time discovering which was which.

It was in the woods here along Camp Branch that Bill White, my grandfather's Negro hired hand, taught me to hunt squirrels. Bill lived in a little tin-roofed house on up nearer the head of the hollow. And this was, I suppose more than any other place, his hunting ground. It was the place of his freedom, where he could move without subservience, without considering who he was or who anybody else was. On late summer mornings, when it was too wet to work, I would follow him into the woods. As soon as we stepped in under the trees he would become silent and absolutely attentive to the life of the place. He was a good teacher and an exacting one. The rule seemed to be that if I wanted to stay with him, I had to make it possible for him to forget I was there. I was to make no noise. If I did he would look back and make a downward emphatic gesture with his hand, as explicit as writing: Be quiet, or go home. He would see a squirrel crouched in a fork or lying along the top of a branch, and indicate with a grin and a small jerk of his head where I should look; and then wait, while I, conscious of being watched and demanded upon, searched it out for myself. He taught me to look and to listen and to be quiet. I wonder if he knew the value of such teaching or the rarity of such a teacher.

In the years that followed I hunted often here alone. And later in these same woods I experienced my first obscure dissatisfactions with hunting. Though I could not have put it into words then, the sense had come to me that hunting as I knew it—the eagerness to kill something I did not need to eat—was an artificial relation to the place, when what I was beginning to need, just as inarticulately then, was a relation that would be deeply natural and meaningful. That was a time of great uneasiness and restlessness for me. It would be the fall of the year, the leaves would be turning, and ahead of me would be another year of school. There would be confusions about girls and ambitions, the wordless hurried feeling that time and events and my own nature were pushing me toward what I was going to be—and I had no notion what it was, or how to prepare.

And then there were years when I did not come here at all—when these places and their history were in my mind, and part of me, in places thousands of miles away. And now I am here again, changed from what I was, and still changing. The future is no more certain to me now than it ever was, though its risks are clearer, and so are my own desires: I am the father of two young children whose lives are hostages given to the future. Because of them and because of events in the world, life seems more fearful and difficult to me now than ever before. But it is also more inviting, and I am constantly aware of its nearness to joy. Much of the interest and excitement that I have in my life now has come from the deepening, in the years since my return here, of my relation to this countryside that is my native place. For in spite of all that has happened to me in other places, the great change and the great possibility of change in my life has been in my sense of this place. The major difference is perhaps only that I have grown able to be wholeheartedly present here. I am able to sit and be quiet at the foot of some tree here in this woods along Camp Branch, and feel a deep peace, both in the place and in my awareness of it, that not too long ago I was not conscious of the possibility of. This peace is partly in being free of the suspicion that pursued me for most of my life, no matter where I was, that there was perhaps another place I *should* be, or would be happier or better in; it is partly in the increasingly articulate consciousness of being here, and of the significance and importance of being here.

After more than thirty years I have at last arrived at the candor necessary to stand on this part of the earth that is so full of my own history and so much damaged by it, and ask: What *is* this place? What is in it? What is its nature? How should men live in it? What must I do?

I have not found the answers, though I believe that in partial and fragmentary ways they have begun to come to me. But the questions are more important than their answers. In the final sense they *have* no answers. They are like the questions—they are perhaps the same questions—that were the discipline of Job. They are a part of the necessary enactment of humility, teaching a man what his importance is, what his responsibility is, and what his place is, both on the earth and in the order of things. And though the answers must always come obscurely and in fragments, the questions must be persistently asked. They are fertile questions. In their implications and effects, they are moral and aesthetic and, in the best and fullest sense, practical. They promise a relationship to the world that is decent and preserving.

They are also, both in origin and effect, religious. I am uneasy with the term, for such religion as has been openly practiced in this part of the world has promoted and fed upon a destructive schism between body and soul, heaven and earth. It has encouraged people to believe that the world is of no importance, and that their only obligation in it is to submit to certain churchly formulas in order to get to heaven. And so the people who might have been expected to care most selflessly for the world have had their minds turned elsewhere—to a pursuit of "salvation" that was really only another form of gluttony and self-love, the desire to perpetuate their own small lives beyond the life of the world. The heaven-bent have abused the earth thoughtlessly, by inattention, and their negligence has permitted and encouraged others to abuse it deliberately. Once the creator was removed from the creation, divinity became only a remote abstraction, a social weapon in the hands of the religious institutions. This split in public values produced or was accompanied by, as it was bound to be, an equally artificial and ugly division in people's lives, so that a man, while pursuing heaven with the sublime appetite he thought of as his soul, could turn his heart against his neighbors and his hands against the world. For these reasons, though I know that my questions *are* religious, I dislike having to *say* that they are.

But when I ask them my aim is not primarily to get to heaven. Though heaven is certainly more important than the earth if all they say about it is true, it is still morally incidental to it and dependent on it, and I can only imagine it and desire it in terms of what I know of the earth. And so my questions do not aspire beyond the earth. They aspire *toward* it and *into* it. Perhaps they aspire *through* it. They are religious because they are asked at the limit of what I know; they acknowledge mystery and honor its presence in the creation; they are spoken in reverence for the order and grace that I see, and that I trust beyond my power to see.

The stream has led me down to an old barn built deep in the hollow to house the tobacco once grown on those abandoned fields. Now it is surrounded by the trees that have come back on every side—a relic, a fragment of another time, strayed out of its meaning. This is the last of my historical landmarks. To here, my walk has had insistent overtones of memory and history. It has been a movement of consciousness through knowledge, eroding and shaping, adding and wearing away. I have descended like the water of the stream through what I know of myself, and now that I have there is a little more to know. But here at the barn, the old roads and the cow paths—the formal connections with civilization —come to an end.

I stoop between the strands of a barbed-wire fence, and in that movement I go out of time into timelessness. I come into a wild place. I walk along the foot of a slope that was once cut bare of trees, like all the slopes of this part of the country—but long ago; and now the woods is established again, the ground healed, the trees grown big, their trunks rising clean, free of undergrowth. The place has a serenity and dignity that one feels immediately; the creation is whole in it and unobstructed. It is free of the strivings and dissatisfactions, the partialities and imperfections of places under the mechanical dominance of men. Here, what to a housekeeper's eye might seem disorderly is nonetheless orderly and within order; what might seem arbitrary or accidental is included in the design of the whole as if by intention; what might seem evil or violent is a comfortable member of the household. Where the creation is whole nothing is extraneous. The presence of the creation here makes this a holy place, and it is as a pilgrim that I have come—to give the homage of awe and love, to submit to mystification. It is the creation that has attracted me, its perfect interfusion of life and design. I have made myself its follower and its apprentice.

One early morning last spring, I came and found the woods floor strewn with bluebells. In the cool sunlight and the lacy shadows of the spring woods the blueness of those flowers, their elegant shape, their delicate fresh scent kept me standing and looking. I found a rich delight in them that I cannot describe and that I will never forget. Though I had been familiar for years with most of the spring woods flowers, I had never seen these and had not known they grew here. Looking at them, I felt a strange feeling of loss and sorrow that I had never seen them before. But I was also exultant that I saw them now—that they were here.

For me, in the thought of them will always be the sense of the joyful surprise with which I found them—

the sense that came suddenly to me then that the world is blessed beyond my understanding, more abundantly than I will ever know. What lives are still ahead of me here to be discovered and exulted in, tomorrow, or in twenty years? What wonder will be found here on the morning after my death? Though as a man I inherit great evils and the possibility of great loss and suffering, I know that my life is blessed and graced by the yearly flowering of the bluebells. How perfect they are! In their presence I am humble and joyful. If I were given all the learning and all the methods of my race I could not make one of them, or even imagine one. Solomon in all his glory was not arrayed like one of these. It is the privilege and the labor of the apprentice of creation to come with his imagination into the unimaginable, and with his speech into the unspeakable.

III

On weekends the Air Force reservists practice war. Their jet fighters come suddenly over the crest of the hill into the opening of the valley, very low, screeching insistently into our minds—perfecting deadliness. We can see the rockets nestling under their wings. They do not represent anything I understand as my own or that I identify with. Unable to imagine myself flying one or employing one for any of my purposes, I am left with the alternative of imagining myself their target. They strike fear into me. I fear them, I think, with the same fear—though not, certainly, with the same intensity—with which they are feared in the villages and the rice paddies of Vietnam. I am afraid that nothing I value can withstand them. I am unable to believe that what I most hope for can be served by them.

☆

On weekends, too, the hunters come out from the cities to kill for pleasure such game as has been able to survive the constraints and destructions of the human economy, the highway traffic, the poison sprays. They come weighted down with expensive clothes and equipment, all purchased for the sake of a few small deaths in a country they neither know nor care about. We hear their guns, and see their cars parked at lane ends and on the roadsides.

☆

Sometimes I can no longer think in the house or in the garden or in the cleared fields. They bear too much resemblance to our failed human history—failed, because it has led to this human present that is such a bitterness and a trial. And so I go to the woods. As I enter in under the trees, dependably, almost at once, and by nothing I do, things fall into place. I enter an order that does not exist outside, in the human spaces. I feel my life take its place among the lives—the trees, the annual plants, the animals and birds, the living of all these and the dead—that go and have gone to make the life of the earth. I am less important than I thought, the human race is less important than I thought. I rejoice in that. My mind loses its urgings, senses its nature, and is free. The forest grew here in its own time, and so I will live, suffer and rejoice, and die in my own time. There is nothing that I may decently hope for that I cannot reach by patience as well as by anxiety. The hill, which is a part of America, has killed no one in the service of the American government. Then why should I, who am a fragment of the hill? I wish to be as peaceable as my land, which does no violence, though it has been the scene of violence and has had violence done to it.

How, having a consciousness, an intelligence, a human spirit—all the vaunted equipment of my race—can I humble myself before a mere piece of the earth and speak of myself as its fragment? Because my mind transcends the hill only to be filled with it, to comprehend it a little, to know that it lives on the hill in time as well as in place, to recognize itself as the hill's fragment.

The false and truly belittling transcendence is ownership. The hill has had more owners than its owners have had years—they are grist for its mill. It has had few friends. But I wish to be its friend, for I think it serves its friends well. It tells them they are fragments of its life. In its life they transcend their years.

☆

The most exemplary nature is that of the topsoil. It is very Christ-like in its passivity and beneficence, and in the penetrating energy that issues out of its peaceableness. It increases by experience, by the passage of seasons over it, growth rising out of it and returning to it, not by ambition or aggressiveness. It is enriched by all things that die and enter into it. It keeps the past, not as history or as memory, but as richness, new possibility. Its fertility is always building up out of death into promise. Death is the bridge or the tunnel by which its past enters its future.

☆

Ownership presumes that only man lives in time, and that the hill is merely present, merely a place. But the poet who lives, heeded or not, within the owner knows that the hill is also taking place. It is as alive as its owner. The two lives go side by side in time together, and ultimately they are the same.

☆

To walk in the woods, mindful only of the *physical* extent of it, is to go perhaps as owner, or as knower, confident of one's own history and of one's own importance. But to go there, mindful as well of its temporal extent, of the age of it, and of all that led up to the present life of it, and of all that will probably follow it, is to feel oneself a flea in the pelt of a great living thing, the discrepancy between its life and one's own so great that it cannot be imagined. One has come into the presence of mystery. After all the trouble one has taken to be a modern man, one has come back under the spell of a primitive awe, wordless and humble.

☆

In the centuries before its settlement by white men, among the most characteristic and pleasing features of the floor of this valley, and of the stream banks on its slopes, were the forests and the groves of great beech trees. With their silver bark and their light graceful foliage, turning gold in the fall, they were surely as lovely as any forests that ever grew on earth. I think so because I have seen their diminished descendants, which have returned to stand in the wasted places that we have so quickly misused and given up. But those old forests are all gone. We will never know them as they were. We have driven them beyond the reach of our minds, only a vague hint of their presence returning to haunt us, as though in dreams—a fugitive rumor of the nobility and beauty and abundance of the squandered maidenhood of our world—so that, do what we will, we will never quite be satisfied ever again to be here.

The country, as we have made it by the pretense that we can do without it as soon as we have completed its metamorphosis into cash, no longer holds even the possibility of such forests, for the topsoil that they made and stood upon, like children piling up and trampling underfoot the fallen leaves, is no longer here.

It is thought that the beech forests of the Midwest, in the time before the white invasion, produced an annual nut crop of a billion bushels. Suppose that early in our history we had learned, like the Indians, to make use of this bounty, and of the rest of the natural produce of the country. We would have been unimaginably different, and would have been less in need of forgiveness. Instead of asking what was already here that might be of use to us, we hastened to impose on the face of the new country, like the scraps and patches of a collage, the fields and the crop rows and the fences of Europe. We destroyed the abundance that lay before us simply by being unwilling or unable to acknowledge that it was there. We did not know where we were, and to avoid the humility and the labor of our ignorance, we pretended to be where we had come from. And so there is a sense in which we are still not here. Because we have ignored the place we have come to, our presence here remains curiously accidental, as though we came by misapprehension or mistake, like birds driven out to sea by a storm.

We still want to be Europeans. We have abandoned Europe only reluctantly and only by necessity. We tried for two hundred years to grow the European grape here, without success, before turning to the development of the native vines that abounded in variety and in health in all parts of the country.

☆

There is an ominous—perhaps a fatal—presumptuousness, like the *hybris* of the ancient kings, in living in a place by the *imposition* on it of one's preconceived or inherited ideas and wishes. And that is the way we white people have lived in America throughout our history, and it is the way our history now teaches us to live here.

Surely there could be a more indigenous life than we have. There could be a consciousness that would establish itself on a place by understanding its nature and learning what is potential in it. A man ought to study the wilderness of a place before applying to it the ways he learned in another place. Thousands of acres of hill land, here and in the rest of the country, were wasted by a system of agriculture that was fundamentally alien to it. For more than a century, here, the steepest hillsides were farmed, by my forefathers and their neighbors, as if they were flat, and as if this was not a country of heavy rains. And that symbolizes well enough how alien we remain, in our behavior and in our thoughts, to our country. We haven't yet, in any meaningful sense, arrived in these places that we declare we own. We undertook the privilege of the virgin abundance of this land without any awareness at all that we undertook at the same time a responsibility toward it. That responsibility has never yet impressed itself upon our character; its absence in us is signified on the land by scars.

Until we understand what the land is, we are at odds with everything we touch. And to come to that understanding it is necessary, even now, to leave the regions of our conquest—the cleared fields, the towns and cities, the highways—and re-enter the woods. For only there can a man encounter the silence and the darkness of his own absence. Only in this silence and darkness can he recover the sense of the world's longevity, of its ability to thrive without him, of his inferiority to it and his dependence on it. Perhaps then, having heard that silence and seen that darkness, he will grow humble before the place and begin to take it in—to learn *from it* what it is. As its sounds come into his hearing, and its lights and colors come into his vision, and its odors come into his nostrils, then he may come into *its* presence as he never has before, and he will arrive in his place and will want to remain. His life will grow out of the ground like the other lives of the place, and take its place among them. He will be *with* them—neither ignorant of them, nor indifferent to them, nor against them—and so at last he will grow to be native-born. That is, he must re-enter the silence and the darkness, and be born again.

One winter night nearly twenty years ago I was in the woods with the coon hunters, and we were walking toward the dogs, who had moved out to the point of the bluff where the valley of Cane Run enters the valley of the river. The footing was difficult, and one of the hunters was having trouble with his lantern. The flame would "run up" and smoke the globe, so that the light it gave obscured more than it illuminated, an obstacle between his eyes and the path. At last he cursed it and flung it down into a hollow. Its little light went looping down through the trees and disappeared, and there was a distant tinkle of glass as the globe shattered. After that he saw better and went along the bluff easier than before, and lighter, too.

Not long ago, walking up there, I came across his old lantern lying rusted in the crease of the hill, half buried already in the siftings of the slope, and I let it lie. But I've kept the memory that it renewed. I have made it one of my myths of the hill. It has come to be truer to me now than it was then.

For I have turned aside from much that I knew, and have given up much that went before. What will not bring me, more certainly than before, to where I am is of no use to me. I have stepped out of the clearing into the woods. I have thrown away my lantern, and I can see the dark.

☆

In order to know the hill it is necessary to slow the mind down, imaginatively at least, to the hill's pace. For the hill, like Valery's sycamore, is a voyager standing still. Never moving a step, it travels through years, seasons, weathers, days and nights. These are the measures of its time, and they alter it, marking their passage on it as on a man's face. The hill has never observed a Christmas or an Easter or a Fourth of July. It has nothing to do with a dial or a calendar. Time is told in it mutely and immediately, with perfect accuracy, as it is told by the heart in the body. Its time is the birth and the flourishing and the death of the many lives that are its life.

☆

The hill is like an old woman, all her human obligations met, who sits at work day after day, in a kind of rapt leisure, at an intricate embroidery. She has time for all things. Because she does not expect ever to be finished, she is endlessly patient with details. She perfects flower and leaf, feather and song, adorning the briefest life in great beauty as though it were meant to last forever.

☆

In the early spring I climb up through the woods to an east-facing bluff where the bloodroot bloom in scattered colonies around the foot of the rotting monument of a tree trunk. The sunlight is slanting, clear, through the leafless branches. The flowers are white and perfect, delicate as though shaped in air and water. There is a fragility about them that communicates how short a time they will last. There is some subtle bond between them and the dwindling great trunk of the dead tree. There comes on me a pressing wish to imitate them and so preserve them. But I know that what draws me to them would not pass over into anything I can *do*. They will be lost. In a few days none will be here. Suddenly I want to be, I don't know which, a worshiper or a god.

☆

Coming upon a mushroom growing out of a pad of green moss between the thick roots of an oak, the sun and the dew still there together, I have felt my mind irresistibly become small, to inhabit that place, leaving me standing vacant and bewildered, like a boy whose captured field mouse has just leaped out of his hand.

☆

As I slowly fill with the knowledge of this place, and sink into it, I come to the sense that my life here is inexhaustible, that its possibilities lie rich behind and ahead of me, that when I am dead it will not be used up.

☆

Too much that we do is done at the expense of something else, or somebody else. There is some intransigent destructiveness in us. My days, though I think I know better, are filled with a thousand irritations, worries, regrets for what has happened and fears for what may, trivial duties, meaningless torments—as destructive of my life as if I wanted to be dead. Take today for what it is, I counsel myself. Let it be enough.

And I dare not, for fear that if I do, yesterday will infect tomorrow. We are in the habit of contention— against the world, against each other, against ourselves.

It is not from ourselves that we will learn to be better than we are.

☆

In spite of all the talk about the law of tooth and fang and the struggle for survival, there is in the lives of the animals and birds a great peacefulness. It is not all fear and flight, pursuit and killing. That is part of it, certainly; and there is cold and hunger; there is the likelihood that death, when it comes, will be violent. But there is peace, too, and I think that the intervals of peace are frequent and prolonged. These are the times when the creature rests, communes with himself or with his kind, takes pleasure in being alive.

This morning while I wrote I was aware of a fox squirrel hunched in the sunlight on a high elm branch beyond my window. The night had been frosty, and now the warmth returned. He stayed there a long time, warming and grooming himself. Was he not at peace? Was his life not pleasant to him then?

I have seen the same peacefulness in a flock of wood ducks perched above the water in the branches of a fallen beech, preening and dozing in the sunlight of an autumn afternoon. Even while they dozed they had about them the exquisite alertness of wild things. If I had shown myself they would have been instantly in the air. But for the time there was no alarm among them, and no fear. The moment was whole in itself, deeply satisfying both to them and to me.

Or the sense of it may come with watching a flock of cedar waxwings eating wild grapes in the top of the woods on a November afternoon. Everything they do is leisurely. They pick the grapes with a curious deliberation, comb their feathers, converse in high windy whistles. Now and then one will fly out and back in a sort of dancing flight full of whimsical flutters and turns. They are like farmers loafing in their own fields on Sunday. Though they have no Sundays, their days are full of sabbaths.

☆

One clear fine morning in early May, when the river was flooded, my friend and I came upon four rough-winged swallows circling over the water, which was still covered with frail wisps and threads of mist from the cool night. They were bathing, dipping down to the water until they touched the still surface with a little splash. They wound their flight over the water like the graceful falling loops of a fine cord. Later they perched on a dead willow, low to the water, to dry and groom themselves, the four together. We paddled the canoe almost within reach of them before they flew. They were neat, beautiful, gentle birds. Sitting there preening in the sun after their cold bath, they communicated a sense of domestic integrity, the serenity of living within order. We didn't belong within the order of the events and needs of their day, and so they didn't notice us until they had to.

☆

But there is not only peacefulness, there is joy. And the joy, less deniable in its evidence than the peacefulness, is the confirmation of it. I sat one summer evening and watched a great blue heron make his descent from the top of the hill into the valley. He came down at a measured deliberate pace, stately as always, like a dignitary going down a stair. And then, at a point I judged to be midway over the river, without at all varying his wingbeat he did a backward turn in the air, a loop-the-loop. It could only have been a gesture of pure exuberance, of joy—a speaking of his sense of the evening, the day's fulfillment, his descent homeward. He made just the one slow turn, and then flew on out of sight in the direction of a slew farther down in the bottom. The movement was incredibly beautiful, at once exultant and stately, a benediction on the evening and on the river and on me. It seemed so perfectly to confirm the presence of a free nonhuman joy in the world—a joy I feel a great need to believe in—that I had the skeptic's impulse to doubt that I had seen it. If I had, I thought, it would be a sign of the presence of something heavenly in the earth. And then, one evening a year later, I saw it again.

☆

Every man is followed by a shadow which is his death—dark, featureless, and mute. And for every man there is a place where his shadow is clarified and is made his reflection, where his face is mirrored in the ground. He sees his source and his destiny, and they are acceptable to him. He becomes the follower of what pursued him. What hounded his track becomes his companion.

That is the myth of my search and my return.

☆

I have been walking in the woods, and have lain down on the ground to rest. It is the middle of October, and around me, all through the woods, the leaves are quietly sifting down. The newly fallen leaves make a dry, comfortable bed, and I lie easy, coming to rest within myself as I seem to do nowadays only when I am in the woods.

And now a leaf, spiraling down in wild flight, lands on my shirt front at about the third button below the collar. At first I am bemused and mystified by the coincidence—that the leaf should have been so hung, weighted and shaped, so ready to fall, so nudged loose and slanted by the breeze, as to fall where I, by the same delicacy of circumstance, happened to be lying. The event, among all its ramifying causes and considerations, and finally its mysteries, begins to take on the magnitude of history. Portent begins to dwell in it.

And suddenly I apprehend in it the dark proposal of the ground. Under the fallen leaf my breastbone burns with imminent decay. Other leaves fall. My body begins its long shudder into humus. I feel my substance escape me, carried into the mold by beetles and worms. Days, winds, seasons pass over me as I sink under the leaves. For a time only sight is left to me, a passive awareness of the sky overhead, birds crossing, the mazed interreaching of the treetops, the leaves falling—and then that, too, sinks away. It is acceptable to me, and I am at peace.

When I move to go, it is as though I rise up out of the world.

ABOUT THE NATIONAL AUDUBON SOCIETY

Reflecting broadening perspectives and deepening concern about the dangers to the environment, the Audubon Society adopted a restatement of their objectives: *To promote the conservation of wildlife and the natural environment, and to educate man regarding his relationship with, and his place within, the natural environment as an ecological system.* Action and education, not appreciation and enjoyment of nature alone.

Audubon is the magazine of the Society. It is published bimonthly—and has been for 71 years. *Audubon's* field editors and contributors await assignment to any conservation battlefield in the world. No despoiler is above concern —neither biggest government nor biggest business.

A $10 individual membership in the National Audubon Society brings you six issues of *Audubon*. You will in turn be supporting the Society's broad program of conservation education and environmental action. You will be making a commitment to a cause—the Audubon cause, and yours as well.

National Audubon Society
1130 Fifth Avenue
New York, N.Y. 10028

I would like to receive a year's six issues of *Audubon*, and to support, through my annual membership, the programs of the society.
I prefer: ☐ a $10 individual membership
☐ a $12.50 family membership

Name: _____

Address: _____

City: _____ State: _____ Zip: _____

☐ I have enclosed my check or money order.
☐ Please send me a bill.

*How to Avoid Poisoning Ourselves
Daily With the Food We Eat*

THE BASIC BOOK OF ORGANIC GARDENING

Edited by Robert Rodale

Now the long-established *Organic Gardening* Magazine and Ballantine Books have produced an original book to guide the unknowledgeable gardener to healthy living through gardening in nature's own way—without pesticides and artificial fertilizers. All the basic information is here:

> What organic gardening is.
>
> Where organic gardening supplies can be obtained.
>
> How to prepare the soil, compost, mulch, etc.
>
> Why gardening organically is essential to the protection of the environment.

An *Organic Gardening*®/Ballantine Book $1.25

To order by mail send price of book plus 5¢ for postage to Dept. CS, Ballantine Books, 36 West 20th Street, N. Y., N. Y. 10003

"A local classic . . ."—Wallace Stegner

ISLAND IN THE SOUND

by Hazel Heckman

Barely a pencil dot on the map—that is how a modern world would regard Anderson Island. Hazel Heckman brings it to life in this warm and loving look at the island and its people. It is a place rich with tradition and friendship. ISLAND IN THE SOUND is a unique chronicle of a vanishing way of life.